THE
YORKSHIRE PUDDING
COOKBOOK

HarperCollins*Publishers*
1 London Bridge Street
London SE1 9GF

www.harpercollins.co.uk

HarperCollins*Publishers*
1st Floor, Watermarque Building, Ringsend Road
Dublin 4, Ireland

First published by HarperCollins*Publishers* 2021

1 3 5 7 9 10 8 6 4 2

© HarperCollins*Publishers* 2021
Photographs © Joff Lee 2021
Food stylist: Mari Williams
Prop stylist: Max Robinson

Heather Thomas asserts the moral right to be identified as the author of this work

A catalogue record of this book is available from the British Library

ISBN 978-0-00-848589-4

Printed and bound in Latvia

MIX
Paper from
responsible sources
FSC™ C007454

FSC
www.fsc.org

THE
YORKSHIRE PUDDING
COOKBOOK

HEATHER THOMAS

HarperCollins*Publishers*

CONTENTS

//

INTRODUCTION

Who would have thought it? The humble Yorkshire pudding, made with flour, milk and eggs, has been elevated to a new culinary star. This centuries-old staple dish, which is traditionally eaten with the British Sunday roast, has travelled far beyond the borders of the United Kingdom, and even the United States now has its own annual Yorkshire Pudding Day every October.

HISTORY

The first recipe in print for the Yorkshire pudding was way back in 1747 in Hannah Glasse's cookery book: *The Art of Cookery Made Plain and Easy*. Before this, it was usually called a 'dripping pudding' as it consisted of a pan of batter that was cooked below the roasting meat. As the spit turned, the juices and fat ran out of the joint and dripped onto the pudding below.

The traditional Yorkshire pudding was cooked in a single roasting pan, then cut into slabs or wedges and served with gravy as an appetizer before the main meat course, unlike today when it is usually eaten as a 'side' on the same plate as the meat and vegetables. However, serving it first, on its own, filled people up, making the more expensive main course of meat stretch further. It has now moved on from its humble beginnings and is more often served in individual portions or filled with meaty or vegetarian sausages as a 'toad in the hole'.

POPOVERS

The Yorkshire batter crossed the pond to America over 100 years ago, and crisp 'popovers' became a popular choice for breakfasts, brunches, desserts and snacks right across the States, especially on the East Coast. These infinitely versatile Yorkshire bites can be sweet or savoury, dusted with spices and sugar, drizzled with syrup or flavoured with cheese, hot chillies, herbs, fruit and spices. They are called popovers because the batter rises and swells as it cooks and pops over the edge of the top of the tin.

While popovers flourished in America, the one-pan Yorkshire never really took off or, at least, not until now, when it is fast becoming an Instagram star... As Ogden Nash famously said:

'Let's call Yorkshire Pudding
A fortunate blunder:
It's a sort of popover
That turned and popped under.'

You can enjoy light, buttery popovers any time of the day with butter and jam, or fruit and whipped cream. Or make them for breakfast with bacon, sausages, ham, mushrooms and tomatoes. Serve as a hot tasty snack, piquant with cheese and speckled with herbs, or as a dessert or teatime treat, oozing with chocolate, Nutella or fruit. We've got so many delicious recipes.

THE SCIENCE

There is nothing complicated about Yorkshire puddings and popovers. Made from eggs, flour and milk (sometimes with added butter for popovers), they rise spectacularly when they are cooked in a hot oven to a billowing, puffy, crisp, golden brown wonder. The Royal Society of Chemistry has decreed that to be classified as an authentic Yorkshire pudding, it has to be over 10cm (4 inches) tall, and many people worry about whether their batter will rise enough. However, if you follow our simple fail-safe guidelines and tips, there's no need to get anxious about soggy Yorkshires and popovers that don't pop.

The secret to success is steam. Yorkshires and popovers don't need yeast, baking powder or bicarbonate of soda (baking soda) to help them rise. But it is important to have:

• The right consistency of batter.

• The right liquid to flour ratio.

• The right flour – plain (all-purpose) is best.

• A preheated hot oven at the right temperature.

• ... lots of steam.

With their crisp exterior crust and soft inner heart, popovers and Yorkshires are best eaten hot and fresh from the oven. This book shows you how to make them turn out perfectly every time. There is practical advice and tips on:

• How to make them crisp.

• How to make them rise.

• The best pans to use.

• The best flavourings

• The best stuffings.

• What to serve them with.

SO VERSATILE

The hollowed-out cup shape of the Yorkshire can hold gravy, sauces and fillings of meat, fish, vegetables, fruit, eggs and custard. Make the puddings large, small or mini; or transform them into one-pan tray bakes, wraps, pizzas, blinis, canapés, burritos, tacos and even burgers. Use any leftover batter for pancakes and crêpes – it never goes to waste.

We have recipes for everything in this unique book, from traditional Yorkshire puddings, toads and popovers to Japanese takoyaki, breakfast pancakes, loaded individual puddings, festive Yorkshires, 'profiteroles' and even apple crumble Yorkshires and Mexican chilli and chocolate popovers. They are all quick and easy to make, and there are lots of delicious vegetarian options – there's even a vegan pudding batter. And it's perfectly easy to replace the milk with your preferred non-dairy milk substitute if you need a dairy-free batter. You will be spoilt for choice.

THE BASICS

TRADITIONAL YORKSHIRE PUDDING

//

Basic batter recipes always feature the same four ingredients – flour, salt, eggs and milk, plus fat in the bottom of the pan to crisp the base of the pudding. For a richer, softer pudding, you can use all milk; for a crispier pudding, you can try using a 50:50 mixture of milk and water. If you're making a pudding to accompany a roast, use some of the hot beef, lamb, pork or chicken fat, and save any leftover fat or dripping in a sealed container to keep in the fridge. Vegetarians and vegans can use olive or sunflower oil instead. Any fat will work provided that it is smoking hot when you pour the batter into the pan. It is customary to let the batter rest for 15–30 minutes before cooking it, but if you're in a hurry, don't worry, just go ahead and cook the Yorkshire immediately. It probably won't make any difference to the finished pudding.

SERVES 4–6
PREP 10 MINUTES
STAND 15–30 MINUTES
COOK 25–30 MINUTES

250g (9oz/2½ cups) plain (all-purpose) flour
¼ tsp salt
4 large free-range eggs, beaten
300ml (½ pint/1¼ cups) milk
3 tbsp meat dripping or vegetable oil

Preheat the oven to 220°C (200°C fan)/425°F/gas 7.

Sift the flour and salt into a bowl and make a well in the centre. Add the eggs with a little of the milk. Beat together, then gradually beat in the rest of the milk until you have a smooth batter without any lumps and the consistency of thin cream. Transfer to a jug and set aside to stand for 15–30 minutes.

Put the meat dripping or oil in a large roasting pan and place on a high shelf in the hot oven for 5–10 minutes, or until the fat is hissing, sizzling and smoking.

Quickly pour the batter into the hot pan and place in the oven. Cook for 25–30 minutes, or until well-risen, crisp and golden brown. Do not open the oven door while the pudding is cooking or it may collapse.

Remove from the oven and cut into slabs to eat immediately.

Tip: You can beat the batter by hand, use a hand-held electric whisk or make it in a blender or food processor.

INDIVIDUAL YORKSHIRE PUDDINGS

Individual Yorkshires are crispier and crunchier than a large one, which is always softer in the middle. You have various options regarding which size pans you use. I usually use a deep 12-hole muffin or cupcake pan but you could make larger individual Yorkies in a shallower 4-cup Yorkshire pudding pan.

MAKES 12
PREP 10 MINUTES
STAND 15–30 MINUTES
COOK 20–25 MINUTES

250g (9oz/2½ cups) plain (all-purpose) flour
¼ tsp salt
4 large free-range eggs, beaten
300ml (½ pint/1¼ cups) milk
12 tsp meat dripping or vegetable oil

Preheat the oven to 220°C (200°C fan)/425°F/gas 7.

Make the batter: sift the flour and salt into a bowl and make a well in the centre. Add the eggs with a little of the milk. Beat with a wooden spoon or hand-held electric whisk, then gradually beat in the rest of the milk until you have a smooth batter without any lumps and the consistency of thin cream. Alternatively, use a blender or food processor. Transfer the batter to a jug and set aside to stand for 15–30 minutes.

Put 1 teaspoon meat dripping or oil in each cup of a 12-hole muffin pan and place on a high shelf in the hot oven for about 5–10 minutes, or until the fat is hissing, sizzling and smoking.

Quickly pour the batter into the cups of the hot pan and place in the oven. Cook for 20–25 minutes, or until the puddings are well-risen, crisp and golden brown. Do not open the oven door while the puddings are cooking or they may collapse.

Remove from the oven and serve immediately.

VEGAN YORKSHIRE PUDDINGS

//

Vegans can make delicious crisp Yorkshires with water or non-dairy milk plus aquafaba
to replace the eggs in a traditional batter.

MAKES 12
PREP 10 MINUTES
STAND 15 MINUTES
COOK 20 MINUTES

250g (9oz/2¼ cups) self-raising
    flour
1½ tsp baking powder
½ tsp salt
¼ tsp turmeric
¼ tsp Dijon mustard (optional)
6 tbsp aquafaba (see tip below)
390ml (13fl oz/1½ cups) water or
    non-dairy milk, e.g. soya
    or almond
8 tbsp vegetable oil

Preheat the oven to 220°C/(200°C fan)/425°F/gas 7.

Sift the flour and baking powder into a bowl and stir in the salt
and turmeric. Make a well in the centre.

In a separate bowl, whisk together the mustard, aquafaba and
water or non-dairy milk. Pour into the well and whisk until you
have a smooth batter that is bubbly but without lumps. Set aside
to rest for 15 minutes.

Divide the oil among the cups in a 12-hole muffin pan and place
on a high shelf in the preheated oven for 5–10 minutes, or until
the fat is sizzling and smoking.

Quickly pour the batter into the cups of the hot pan and place in
the oven. Cook for 20 minutes, or until the puddings are well-
risen, crisp and golden brown. Do not open the oven door while
the puddings are cooking or they may collapse.

Remove from the oven and serve immediately.

Tip: Aquafaba is the liquid from a tin of chickpeas (garbanzos).

CHEDDAR YORKSHIRES

//

There are so many ways of flavouring Yorkshires and making them even more delicious (see the list of ideas opposite) but cheese is probably the favourite.

MAKES 12
PREP 10 MINUTES
STAND 15–30 MINUTES
COOK 20–25 MINUTES

250g (9oz/2½ cups) plain (all-purpose) flour
¼ tsp salt
4 large free-range eggs, beaten
300ml (½ pint/1¼ cups) milk or milk and water
50g (2oz/½ cup) grated Cheddar cheese
a few snipped chives
12 tsp vegetable oil

Preheat the oven to 220°C (200°C fan)/425°F/gas 7.

Make the batter: sift the flour and salt into a bowl and make a well in the centre. Add the eggs with a little of the liquid. Beat with a wooden spoon or hand-held electric whisk, and then gradually beat in the rest of the liquid until you have a smooth batter without any lumps and the consistency of thin cream. Alternatively, use a blender or food processor.

Transfer the batter to a jug and set aside to stand for about 15–30 minutes, and then gently stir in the cheese and chives.

Put 1 teaspoon oil in each cup of a 12-hole muffin pan and place on a high shelf in the hot oven for 5–10 minutes, or until the fat is hissing, sizzling and smoking.

Quickly pour the batter into the cups of the hot pan and place in the oven. Cook for 20–25 minutes, or until the puddings are well-risen, crisp and golden brown. Do not open the oven door while the puddings are cooking or they may collapse.

Remove from the oven and serve immediately.

VARIATIONS
- Use crumbled goat's cheese instead of Cheddar.
- Use chopped parsley or fresh thyme leaves instead of chives.
- Add a little mustard or Marmite to the batter.

FLAVOURINGS FOR YORKSHIRES

Yorkshires are surprisingly versatile and there are so many ways of making them more flavourful and interesting. Here are some suggestions for ingredients you can add to savoury or sweet batters.

SAVOURY

- Add some grated Cheddar, Parmesan or other hard cheese.

- Add crumbled blue cheese, such as Roquefort or Stilton, or soft, creamy goat's cheese.

- Add crushed garlic or a pinch of garlic salt.

- Add freshly chopped herbs, e.g. rosemary, chives, parsley, sage, marjoram or thyme.

- Add some English, Dijon or honey mustard.

- Add some grated horseradish or Marmite for a distinctive umami flavour.

- Add some crumbled grilled (broiled) crispy bacon or pancetta.

- Add diced chorizo, salami, sausage or black pudding.

- Add diced ham or chopped prosciutto.

- Add diced or thinly sliced red onion and chopped sage.

- Add ground spices: smoked or sweet paprika, cumin, cinnamon, ginger, cardamom or cloves.

- Add diced fresh chillies, crushed dried chilli flakes or bottled jalapeños.

SWEET

- Add vanilla extract or vanilla bean paste.

- Add fresh diced apple and blackberries.

- Add diced stem ginger, ground ginger, cinnamon, cloves, nutmeg or cardamom.

- Add some cocoa and chocolate chips.

- Add some Nutella.

- Add grated lemon, orange or lime zest.

PERFECT POPOVERS

//

You can serve these popovers for tea with butter and preserves – strawberry jam is really good – or for dessert, sprinkled with sugar with berries and cream or yoghurt. Or just eat them instead of bread rolls with hot soup, steak or grilled (broiled) meat.

MAKES 6–10
PREP 10 MINUTES
COOK 30 MINUTES

Note: If you don't have a 6-hole popover pan just use a standard 12-hole muffin pan in which case the quantities given will make approximately 9–10 popovers.

125g (4½oz/1¼ cups) plain (all-purpose) flour
½ tsp salt
3 large free-range eggs
240ml (8fl oz/1 cup) milk
melted butter, for brushing

Preheat the oven to 220°C (200°C fan)/425°F/gas 7.

Make the batter: sift the flour into a bowl and stir in the salt. Beat together the eggs and milk with a balloon whisk or hand-held electric whisk. Gradually add the liquid mixture to the flour, stirring all the time, until you have a smooth batter without lumps.

Place a 6-cup straight-sided popover pan or a 12-cup muffin pan in the hot oven for 5–10 minutes. Remove and brush each cup with the hot melted butter.

Quickly pour the batter into the cups and bake in the oven for 15 minutes. Reduce the heat to 180°C (160°C fan)/350°F/gas 4 and bake for a further 15 minutes, without opening the oven door, or until well-risen, crisp and golden brown. Do not open the oven door while the popovers are cooking or they may collapse.

VARIATIONS
- If you have a sweet tooth, add 2–3 teaspoons caster (superfine) sugar to the mixture.
- Add a few drops of vanilla or almond extract.

FLAVOURINGS FOR POPOVERS

Like Yorkshires, popovers can be savoury or sweet. Here are some ideas for flavourings, toppings, dustings and drizzles to inspire you.

SAVOURY

· Add some grated Parmesan or Pecorino cheese.

· Add crumbled blue cheese

· Add chopped fresh herbs, e.g. rosemary, chives or thyme.

· Add some freshly ground black pepper.

· Add diced fresh chillies or bottled jalapeños.

· Sprinkle some sea salt or grated cheese over the top before cooking.

SWEET

· For sweet popovers, omit the salt and add 1 tablespoon sugar.

· Add a dash of vanilla extract or vanilla bean paste.

· Add a few drops of almond extract or some Amaretto liqueur.

· Add grated lemon, lime or orange zest.

· Add ground spices, e.g. cinnamon, ginger, cardamom, cloves or Chai seasoning.

· Add fresh seasonal berries, e.g. blueberries, raspberries, strawberries, redcurrants and juicy cherries.

· Add chocolate chips, grated chocolate or cocoa.

TOPPINGS, DUSTINGS AND DRIZZLES

· Dust with cocoa powder or icing (confectioner's) sugar.

· Dust with ground cinnamon or nutmeg.

· Drizzle with a fruit coulis or compote.

· Drizzle with chocolate sauce or dulce de leche.

· Drizzle with maple syrup.

· Smear with butter or whipped cream and jam or a fruit conserve.

· Sprinkle with crunchy brown sugar.

· Serve with sliced banana and a caramel sauce.

ONION GRAVY

//

Serve this tasty gravy with Yorkshires, toad in the hole, roast meat, chicken and sausages.
It freezes well in an airtight container for up to 3 months.

**MAKES 360ML (12FL OZ/
1½ CUPS)
PREP 5 MINUTES
COOK 20–25 MINUTES**

3 tbsp olive oil
2 large onions, thinly sliced
1 tbsp plain (all-purpose) flour
300ml (½ pint/1¼ cups) beef,
    chicken or vegetable stock
60ml (2fl oz/¼ cup) balsamic
    vinegar
salt and freshly ground black
    pepper

Heat the olive oil in a frying pan (skillet) set over a low heat. Add the onions and cook for 15 minutes, stirring occasionally, until really tender and starting to caramelize.

Stir in the flour and cook for 1 minute. Stir in the stock and balsamic vinegar and turn the heat up to high. Bring to the boil, stirring, then reduce the heat and let the gravy bubble gently for 4–5 minutes until thickened and smooth.

Season to taste with salt and pepper and transfer to a sauce boat or gravy jug.

VARIATIONS
· Use red onions instead of white.
· Use red wine vinegar or cider vinegar.
· Add some crushed garlic.

MUSHROOM GRAVY

//

This is a great accompaniment to toad in the hole or Yorkshire pudding. To make it vegan-friendly, use vegetable stock and add a dash of soy sauce.

MAKES 420ML (14FL OZ/ 1¾ CUPS)
PREP 10 MINUTES
COOK 30–35 MINUTES

4 tbsp olive oil or meat dripping
1 onion, diced
300g (10oz) mushrooms,
    e.g. white or chestnut, chopped
2 tbsp plain (all-purpose) flour
480ml (16fl oz/2 cups) hot beef,
    chicken or vegetable stock
1 tbsp balsamic vinegar
salt and freshly ground black
    pepper

Heat the oil or dripping in a frying pan (skillet) set over a medium heat. Cook the onion, stirring occasionally, for 10 minutes, or until softened and golden.

Add the mushrooms and cook for 5 minutes, stirring occasionally, until tender and golden brown.

Add the flour and stir well. Cook for 2–3 minutes and then pour in the stock. Stir well to absorb the flour, then add the vinegar and cook for 10–15 minutes, giving it the occasional stir, until reduced and the right consistency for your taste.

Check the seasoning and pour into a sauce boat or gravy jug.

VARIATIONS
- Use porcini or wild mushrooms for extra flavour.
- Add a dash of soy or tamari sauce or some mushroom ketchup.
- Stir in some double (heavy) cream or crème fraîche just before serving.
- Add a pinch of sugar.
- Use dried porcini instead of fresh mushrooms and the soaking water instead of stock.

ROASTED RED ONION AND WINE GRAVY

This rich, smooth gravy is the perfect accompaniment to Yorkshires or toad in the hole.
Any leftover gravy can be kept in the fridge for up to 4 days and reheated, or
frozen for up to 3 months.

**MAKES 420ML (14FL OZ/
1¾ CUPS)
PREP 10 MINUTES
COOK 45–50 MINUTES**

3 red onions, thinly sliced
2 garlic cloves, crushed
3 tbsp olive oil
1 tbsp soft brown sugar
1 tsp Dijon mustard
2 tbsp plain (all-purpose) flour
300ml (½ pint/1¼ cups) red wine
300ml (½ pint/1¼ cups) beef,
   chicken or vegetable stock
salt and freshly ground
   black pepper

Preheat the oven to 200°C (180°C fan)/400°F/gas 6.

Put the onions and garlic in a roasting pan and drizzle with the
olive oil. Season lightly with salt and pepper. Roast in the oven
for 30 minutes, or until the onions are really tender, golden
brown and starting to caramelize.

Place the roasting pan over a medium to high heat on the hob
and stir in the sugar and Dijon mustard, stirring until the sugar
dissolves. Stir in the flour and then add the red wine, stirring well.

Bring to the boil, then reduce the heat to medium and let it
bubble away for 5 minutes, or until the gravy has reduced by half.

Add the stock, increase the heat and bring back to the boil,
stirring. Reduce the heat to medium and simmer for at least
5 minutes, or until the gravy has reduced to a coating
consistency. It should not be too thin. Check the seasoning
and pour into a sauce boat or gravy jug.

VARIATIONS
· Use Madeira or Marsala instead of red wine.
· Add a spoonful of cranberry sauce or apple jelly.
· Flavour with a bay leaf, some sprigs of thyme or rosemary.

BREAKFASTS AND BRUNCHES

FULL ENGLISH YORKSHIRE

Crisp on the outside and soft on the inside, Yorkshire pudding complements the traditional full English meaty sausages, crispy bacon, fried mushrooms and tomatoes.

SERVES 4
PREP 10 MINUTES
COOK 45 MINUTES

4 large pork sausages
3 tbsp olive oil
150g (5oz) button mushrooms
200g (7oz) baby plum or cherry
  tomatoes
4 slices of streaky bacon
salt and freshly ground black
  pepper

BATTER
125g (4½oz/1¼ cups) plain
  (all-purpose) flour
¼ tsp salt
3 large free-range eggs, beaten
300ml (½ pint/1¼ cups) milk

Preheat the oven to 200°C (180°C fan)/400°F/gas 6.

Make the Yorkshire batter: sift the flour and salt into a bowl and whisk in the beaten eggs and a little of the milk. Gradually whisk in the remaining milk until you have a smooth batter without any lumps. Transfer to a jug and leave to stand.

Place the sausages in a large roasting pan and drizzle 1 tablespoon of the olive oil over them. Cook in the preheated oven for 15 minutes, turning them over halfway through.

Add the mushrooms and tomatoes to the pan and drizzle with the remaining oil. Add the bacon and season with salt and pepper. Return to the oven and increase the heat to 220°C (200°C fan)/425°F/gas mark 7. Cook for 5 minutes.

Quickly pour the batter into the hot pan – around the sausages and tomatoes if possible – and return to the oven. Bake for 25 minutes, or until the batter rises and is puffy, crisp and golden brown. Do not open the oven door while the pudding is cooking or it may collapse.

Cut into 4 slabs and place each one on a warm serving plate. Eat immediately while the pudding is piping hot.

Tip: You can prepare the batter in advance or even the night before.

VARIATIONS
- For a vegetarian option use Quorn or any vegetarian meat-free sausages and omit the bacon.
- Use pancetta instead of bacon.
- Add some sliced red (bell) peppers.
- Crack some eggs into the pudding after 20 minutes and cook for 5–10 minutes until set.

BREAKFAST EGGY YORKSHIRES

//

This could well become your favourite breakfast – a crisp golden Yorkshire pudding topped with a fried egg. So simple and utterly delicious!

MAKES 4
PREP 15 MINUTES
STAND 30 MINUTES
COOK 20–25 MINUTES

Note: For the best results, you will need a non-stick deep 4-cup 23cm (9 inch) square Yorkshire pudding pan.

3 tbsp vegetable oil

15g (½oz/1 tbsp) unsalted butter
4 medium free-range eggs
snipped chives, to garnish
maple syrup or ketchup,
    for drizzling

BATTER
125g (4½oz/1¼ cups) plain
    (all-purpose) flour
¼ tsp salt
3 large free-range eggs, beaten
240ml (8fl oz/1 cup) milk

Preheat the oven to 220°C (200°C fan)/425°F/gas 7.

Make the Yorkshire batter: sift the flour and salt into a bowl. Beat the eggs with the milk and pour into the flour, whisking until you have a smooth batter without any lumps. Pour into a jug and leave to stand for at least 30 minutes (overnight, if wished).

Put 1 teaspoon of the oil in each of the cups of the Yorkshire pudding pan and place in the preheated oven for 5–10 minutes, until the oil is smoking and sizzling hot.

Quickly pour the batter into the cups and place in the oven immediately. Bake for 20–25 minutes, or until the batter rises and is puffy, crisp and golden brown. Do not open the oven door while the puddings are cooking or they may collapse.

Meanwhile, towards the end of the cooking time, heat the remaining oil and the butter in a large frying pan (skillet) and fry the eggs until the whites are set but the yolks are still runny.

Remove the Yorkshires and transfer to 4 serving plates. Place a fried egg inside each one and sprinkle with chives. Drizzle with maple syrup or some ketchup and serve immediately.

VARIATIONS
• Sprinkle a few dried chilli flakes over the eggs.
• Add some grated Cheddar cheese.
• Add some chopped spring onions (scallions) or diced red (bell) pepper.
• Add some crumbled crispy bacon.

MEATY BREAKFAST TOAD

This tasty toad in the hole is not for vegetarians or the faint-hearted. It's a very satisfying way to start your day and will keep you going right through the morning. It's particularly good for a weekend breakfast or brunch on a cold winter's day.

SERVES 4
PREP 10 MINUTES
COOK 40–45 MINUTES

4 tbsp olive oil
6 pork and leek sausages, cut into large chunks
175g (6oz) smoked bacon lardons or pancetta cubes
125g (4½oz) mushrooms, sliced or quartered
200g (7oz) black pudding or boudin noir, skinned and crumbled
leaves stripped from a few sprigs of thyme
maple syrup, for drizzling (optional)

BATTER
175g (6oz/1¾ cups) plain (all-purpose) flour
¼ tsp salt
4 large free-range eggs, beaten
420ml (14fl oz/1¾ cups) milk
2 tsp wholegrain mustard

Preheat the oven to 220°C (200°C fan)/425°F/gas 7.

Make the Yorkshire batter: sift the flour and salt into a bowl. Beat the eggs with the milk and mustard and pour into the flour, whisking until you have a smooth batter without any lumps. Pour into a jug and set aside.

Heat 2 tablespoons of the oil in a large frying pan (skillet) set over a medium heat. Cook the sausages, turning occasionally, for 10 minutes and then add the bacon or pancetta together with the mushrooms and black pudding. Cook for 4–5 minutes, or until everything is browned and the mushrooms are tender.

Meanwhile, put the remaining oil in a large roasting pan and place in the preheated oven for 5 minutes or until the oil is sizzling hot.

Transfer the sausages, bacon, black pudding and mushrooms to the pan and sprinkle with the thyme.

Pour the batter into the pan and return to the oven immediately. Cook for 25–30 minutes, or until the batter rises and is puffy, crisp and golden brown. Do not open the oven door while the pudding is cooking or it may collapse.

Slices into wedges and serve immediately, drizzled with maple syrup (if using).

VARIATIONS
- Use diced chorizo, boudin blanc or West Country hog's pudding instead of black pudding.
- Use garlicky Toulouse or Italian country sausages.
- Add some peeled garlic cloves or a sliced red onion.

CHEESY VEGGIE BREAKFAST TOAD

//

This cheesy Yorkshire with succulent garlicky mushrooms is a great vegetarian dish for breakfast, brunch or even supper. To make it more piquant, try adding some mustard or chilli flakes.

SERVES 4
PREP 10 MINUTES
STAND 15 MINUTES
COOK 40–45 MINUTES

4 Portobello or large field
   mushrooms, peeled
4 whole garlic cloves, unpeeled
2–3 tbsp olive oil
salt and freshly ground black
   pepper
grated Cheddar cheese,
   for sprinkling

BATTER
175g (6oz/1¾ cups) plain
   (all-purpose) flour
¼ tsp salt
4 large free-range eggs, beaten
420ml (14fl oz/1¾ cups) milk
50g (2oz/½ cup) grated
   Cheddar cheese
a bunch of chives, snipped

Preheat the oven to 220°C (200°C fan)/425°F/gas 7.

Make the batter: sift the flour and salt into a bowl and make a well in the centre. Whisk in the eggs with a little of the milk, then gradually beat in the rest of the milk until you have a smooth batter without any lumps. Transfer to a jug and leave to stand for at least 15 minutes, then gently stir in the cheese and chives.

Place the mushrooms, open-side up, in a roasting pan. Add the garlic cloves and drizzle with the olive oil. Season with salt and pepper and bake in the preheated oven for 15–20 minutes, or until the mushrooms are cooked and tender. Squeeze the garlic out of the skins and spoon over the mushrooms.

Quickly pour the batter into the hot pan around the mushrooms and return to the oven. Cook for 25 minutes, or until the pudding is well-risen, crisp and golden brown. Do not open the oven door while the pudding is cooking or it may collapse.

Remove from the oven and serve immediately, cut into slabs and sprinkled with grated Cheddar.

VARIATIONS
· Roast some cherry tomatoes alongside the mushrooms.
· Substitute parsley, rosemary or thyme for the chives.
· Try grated Parmesan, Gruyère, Emmenthal or
  Monterey Jack.

BACON BREAKFAST POPOVERS

For a big breakfast, serve these popovers with grilled (broiled) mushrooms and tomatoes. They're best eaten hot from the oven while crisp and puffy and the egg yolks are still runny.

MAKES 6–10
PREP 10 MINUTES
COOK 25–30 MINUTES

Note: If you don't have a 6-hole popover pan just use a standard 12-hole muffin pan in which case the quantities given will make approximately 9–10 popovers.

6–10 tsp vegetable oil
3 slices of lean smoked
   bacon, diced
6–10 medium free-range eggs
   (see Note)
salt and freshly ground black
   pepper

BATTER
125g (4½oz/1¼ cups) plain
   (all-purpose) flour
½ tsp salt
3 large free-range eggs
240ml (8fl oz/1 cup) milk
1 tbsp melted butter

Preheat the oven to 220°C (200°C fan)/425°F/gas 7.

Make the popover batter: sift the flour and salt into a bowl. Whisk together the eggs, milk and melted butter in another bowl. Add to the flour and whisk until you have a smooth batter without any lumps. Transfer to a jug and set aside.

Put 1 teaspoon oil into each cup in a 6-cup popover pan or a 12-cup muffin pan. Place in the oven for 5–10 minutes until the oil is sizzling and starting to smoke.

Quickly divide the diced bacon between the cups in the pan and pour in the batter. Fill each pan about three-quarters full. Return to the oven and cook for 15 minutes. Reduce the heat to 180°C (160°C fan)/350°F/gas 4 and crack an egg into each popover. Pop back into the oven for 10–15 minutes, or until the egg whites are set and the popovers are puffy, crisp and golden. Do not open the oven door while the popovers are cooking or they may collapse.

Turn out the popovers by running a knife around the edge. Season with salt and pepper and serve immediately.

VARIATIONS
- Add some diced mushrooms or chopped herbs.
- Use diced sausage or chorizo instead of bacon.
- Serve with maple syrup or ketchup.

CHEESY HAM POPOVERS

//

This is a really simple and tasty recipe for a weekend family breakfast, or you can enjoy these savoury popovers with a crisp salad for a light lunch.

MAKES 6–10
PREP 10 MINUTES
COOK 30 MINUTES

Note: If you don't have a 6-hole popover pan just use a standard 12-hole muffin pan in which case the quantities given will make approximately 9–10 popovers.

melted butter, for brushing
6 wafer-thin slices of cooked ham, folded over
50g (2oz/½ cup) grated Swiss or Cheddar cheese
freshly ground black pepper

BATTER
125g (4½oz/1¼ cups) plain (all-purpose) flour
½ tsp salt
3 large free-range eggs
240ml (8fl oz/1 cup) milk
1 tbsp melted butter

Preheat the oven to 220°C (200°C fan)/425°F/gas 7.

Make the popover batter: sift the flour and salt into a bowl. Whisk together the eggs, milk and melted butter in another bowl. Add to the flour and whisk until you have a smooth batter without any lumps. Transfer to a jug and set aside.

Generously brush each cup in a 6-cup non-stick popover pan or a 12-cup muffin pan with melted butter. Place in the oven for 5–10 minutes until really hot.

Quickly pour a little batter into each cup, add a folded slice of ham and a little grated cheese, then cover with more batter. Fill each cup about three-quarters full.

Bake in the oven for 15 minutes, then reduce the heat to 180°C (160°C fan)/350°F/gas 4 and bake for a further 15 minutes, or until the popovers are well-risen, puffy and golden brown. Do not open the oven door while the popovers are cooking or they may collapse.

Serve immediately while the popovers are hot and crispy.

VARIATIONS
· Dice some cooked ham instead of using wafer-thin slices.
· Add some diced tomatoes or mushrooms.
· Add some chopped parsley or chives.
· Add a teaspoon honey mustard to the batter.

DOUGHNUT POPOVERS

//

Crisp buttery popovers hot out of the oven and served with good-quality jam are perfect with a mug of coffee for breakfast or a cup of tea in the afternoon when you're feel like something sweet and sustaining.

MAKES 6–10
PREP 10 MINUTES
COOK 30 MINUTES

Note: If you don't have a 6-hole popover pan just use a standard 12-hole muffin pan in which case the quantities given will make approximately 9–10 popovers.

125g (4½oz/1¼ cups) plain (all-purpose) flour
½ tsp salt
3 large free-range eggs
240ml (8fl oz/1 cup) milk
2 tbsp melted butter, plus extra for brushing
caster (superfine) sugar, for sprinkling
raspberry, strawberry, cherry or apricot jam, to serve

Preheat the oven to 220°C (200°C fan)/425°F/gas 7.

Make the popover batter: sift the flour and salt into a bowl. Whisk together the eggs, milk and melted butter in another bowl. Add to the flour and whisk until you have a smooth batter without any lumps. Transfer to a jug and set aside.

Generously brush each cup in a 6-cup popover pan or a 12-cup muffin pan with melted butter. Place in the oven for 5–10 minutes until really hot.

Quickly pour the batter into the cups, so they are about three-quarters full. Bake in the oven for 15 minutes, then reduce the oven temperature to 180°C (160°C fan)/350°F/gas 4 and continue baking for 15 minutes, or until puffy, well-risen and golden brown. Do not open the oven door while the popovers are cooking or they may collapse.

Turn out the popovers and brush lightly with more melted butter. Sprinkle with sugar and serve immediately with plenty of fruity jam. Just tear them in half and place a spoonful of jam in each hollow.

VARIATIONS
· Add some grated orange zest to the batter.
· Serve with fresh berries and crème fraîche or mascarpone.

BLUEBERRY BREAKFAST POPOVERS

//

Instead of blueberry muffins for breakfast, why not treat yourself and try these delicious popovers. They are so quick and easy to make – you can even use a blender or food processor instead of whisking them by hand.

MAKES 6–10
PREP 10 MINUTES
COOK 30 MINUTES

Note: If you don't have a 6-hole popover pan just use a standard 12-hole muffin pan in which case the quantities given will make approximately 9–10 popovers.

100g (4oz/1 cup) blueberries
icing (confectioner's) sugar,
    for dusting

BATTER
125g (4½oz/1¼ cups) plain
    (all-purpose) flour
½ tsp salt
2 tsp caster (superfine) sugar
3 large free-range eggs
240ml (8fl oz/1 cup) milk
2 tbsp melted butter, plus extra
    for brushing
a few drops of vanilla extract

Preheat the oven to 220°C (200°C fan)/425°F/gas 7.

Make the popover batter: sift the flour and salt into a bowl and stir in the sugar. Whisk together the eggs, milk, melted butter and vanilla in another bowl. Add to the flour and whisk until you have a smooth batter without any lumps. Transfer to a jug and set aside.

Generously brush each cup in a 6-cup non-stick popover pan or a 12-cup muffin pan with melted butter. Place in the oven for 5–10 minutes until really hot.

Quickly pour the batter into the cups, so they are about three-quarters full. Divide the blueberries into the cups and bake in the oven for 15 minutes. Reduce the oven temperature to 180°C (160°C fan)/350°F/gas 4 and continue baking for 15 minutes, or until puffy, well-risen and golden brown. Do not open the oven door while the popovers are cooking or they may collapse.

Turn out the popovers and lightly dust with icing sugar. Eat them while they're still hot.

VARIATIONS
· Use frozen blueberries instead of fresh.
· Dust with ground cinnamon.
· Add a little grated lemon or orange zest.
· Use raspberries instead of blueberries.

LIGHT MEALS
AND SIDES

LOADED YORKSHIRES

//

You can cook the Yorkshire puddings fresh for this recipe or reheat some you've already made.
They are great for a light meal or even party food.

MAKES 12
PREP 15 MINUTES
COOK 35 MINUTES

12 Individual Yorkshire Puddings
   (see page 16)
6 slices of streaky bacon
12 ready-to-eat large prunes,
   stoned (pitted)
olive oil, for brushing
gravy and green vegetables,
   to serve

STUFFING BALLS
2 tbsp olive oil
1 tbsp butter
1 large onion, diced
2 garlic cloves, crushed
a few sage leaves, chopped
175g (6oz/3 cups) fresh white
   breadcrumbs
grated zest and juice of 1 lemon
1 large free-range egg, beaten
salt and freshly ground black
   pepper

If you're making the Yorkshires from scratch, preheat the oven, make the batter and cook them as per the recipe on page 16.

When they are cooked or if you aren't cooking the Yorkshires fresh, adjust the heat to 200°C (180°C fan)/400°F/gas 6. Line a baking tray (cookie sheet) with baking parchment.

Meanwhile, make the stuffing balls: Heat the oil and butter in a frying pan (skillet) set over a low heat and cook the onion and garlic, stirring occasionally, for 12–15 minutes, or until softened but not coloured. Stir in the sage and cook for 1 minute.

Remove from the heat and stir in the breadcrumbs, lemon zest and juice. Next stir in the beaten egg to bind the mixture. Season lightly with salt and pepper.

Divide the mixture into 12 portions and, using your hands, roll each one into a ball. Place the balls on the baking tray and bake in the oven for 20 minutes, or until crisp and golden brown.

Meanwhile, stretch out the slices of bacon thinly by running the back of a knife along their length. Cut each one in half and wrap around a prune. Secure with a wooden cocktail stick (toothpick) and brush with a little oil. Place on another baking tray and cook in the oven for 8–10 minutes, until the prunes are warm and the bacon is golden brown and crisp.

Place a stuffing ball and a bacon-wrapped prune in each hot Yorkshire pudding – if you made them in advance, reheat them in a muffin pan or on a baking tray first. Serve immediately with gravy and green vegetables.

SPICY ONION BHAJI YORKSHIRES

///

These spicy individual Yorkshire puddings make a great lunch, side dish or even a snack.
You could also make them in an 18-cup mini muffin pan and serve them as canapés
or with pre-dinner drinks.

MAKES 12
PREP 15 MINUTES
STAND 30 MINUTES
COOK 20–25 MINUTES

2 red onions, thinly sliced
1 red chilli, diced
1 tsp fennel seeds
1 tsp ground turmeric
1 tsp ground cumin
1 tsp ground coriander
½ tsp chilli powder
12 tsp vegetable oil
Indian chutney and pickles,
    to serve

BATTER
125g (4½oz/1¼ cups) plain
    (all-purpose) flour
¼ tsp salt
freshly ground black pepper
3 large free-range eggs, beaten
200ml (7fl oz/scant 1 cup) milk
a handful of coriander
    (cilantro), chopped

Put the onions in a bowl with the chilli, fennel seeds, ground spices and chilli powder. Stir well and set aside for 30 minutes.

Preheat the oven to 220°C (200°C fan)/425°F/gas 7.

Make the batter: sift the flour and salt into a bowl. Add the black pepper and make a well in the centre. Beat in the eggs with a little milk, then gradually beat in the rest of the milk until you have a smooth batter without any lumps. Stir in the coriander and spicy onions. Transfer to a jug and set aside.

Put 1 teaspoon oil in each cup of a 12-hole muffin pan and place in the preheated oven for 5–10 minutes, or until smoking and sizzling.

Quickly ladle the batter into the muffin pan, distributing the onions evenly into the cups. Bake in the oven for about 20–25 minutes, or until well-risen, crisp and golden brown. Do not open the oven door while the puddings are cooking or they may collapse.

Serve immediately with salad and a selection of chutneys and pickles if liked.

VARIATIONS
- Vary the spices: add some paprika, cumin seeds or garam masala.
- Make one large Yorkshire instead of individual ones.
- Use white onions instead of red.

SPINACH FETA TOAD

///

You don't need sausages to make a delicious toad in the hole. Vegetables work just as well.
We have used some traditional Greek flavours here – spinach, dill and feta – to create
a tasty vegetarian lunch.

SERVES 4
PREP 20 MINUTES
COOK 50–60 MINUTES

4 red onions, cut into wedges
3 garlic cloves, unpeeled
4 tbsp olive oil
100g (4oz) spinach leaves,
    trimmed, washed, dried
    and shredded
100g (4oz) feta cheese, crumbled
salt and freshly ground black
    pepper
gravy, to serve

BATTER
175g (6oz/1¾ cups) plain
    (all-purpose) flour
¼ tsp salt
4 large free-range eggs, beaten
420ml (14fl oz/1¾ cups) milk
a few sprigs of parsley or dill,
    finely chopped

Preheat the oven to 190°C (170°C fan)/375°F/gas 5.

Make the batter: sift the flour and salt into a bowl and make
a well in the centre. Beat in the eggs with a little milk, then
gradually beat in the rest of the milk until you have a smooth
batter without any lumps. Transfer to a jug and set aside.

Put the onions and garlic in a large roasting pan and drizzle with
3 tablespoons of the oil. Season with salt and pepper and roast in
the preheated oven for 25–30 minutes, or until the onions are
tender and starting to caramelize. Squeeze the garlic out of the
skins and remove from the pan with the onions. Set aside.

Turn the oven up to 220°C (200°C fan)/425°F/gas 7. Add the
remaining oil to the pan and pop back into the oven for 5–10
minutes until the oil is really hot and sizzling.

Quickly return the onions and garlic to the pan. Scatter with the
spinach and feta and pour the batter over the top. Bake in the
oven for 25–30 minutes, or until well-risen, golden brown and
crisp on top. Do not open the oven door while the pudding is
cooking or it may collapse.

Serve immediately, cut into wedges, with gravy (see pages
23–25).

VARIATIONS
- Add some cubed butternut squash, sweet potato
  or pumpkin.
- Use kale instead of spinach.
- Add some mustard to the Yorkshire batter.

SMOKED SALMON AND DILL YORKSHIRES

///

This pretty dish is perfect for a springtime lunch with friends. Serve it with a crisp salad or some seasonal spring vegetables.

MAKES 12
PREP 15 MINUTES
COOK 20–25 MINUTES

12 tsp vegetable oil
175g (6oz) smoked salmon,
    thinly sliced
lemon wedges, for squeezing

BATTER
175g (6oz/1¾ cups) plain
    (all-purpose) flour
¼ tsp salt
freshly ground black pepper
4 large free-range eggs, beaten
420ml (14fl oz/1¾ cups) milk
1 garlic clove, crushed
a small handful of dill, chopped

PEA PURÉE
150g (5oz/1 cup) frozen peas
120ml (4fl oz/½ cup) crème
    fraîche
1 tbsp horseradish sauce or relish
grated zest of 1 lemon
a squeeze of lemon juice
salt and freshly ground black
    pepper

Preheat the oven to 220°C (200°C fan)/425°F/gas 7.

Make the batter: sift the flour and salt into a bowl. Add the black pepper and make a well in the centre. Beat in the eggs with a little milk, then gradually whisk in the rest of the milk until you have a smooth batter without any lumps. Stir in the garlic and dill, then transfer to a jug and set aside.

Put 1 teaspoon oil in each cup of a 12-hole muffin pan and place in the oven for 5–10 minutes, or until smoking and sizzling.

Quickly ladle the batter into the muffin pan and bake in the oven for 20–25 minutes, or until well-risen, crisp and golden brown. Do not open the oven door while the puddings are cooking or they may collapse.

Meanwhile, bring some water to the boil in a saucepan and tip in the frozen peas. Cook for 3 minutes and drain well.

Put the peas in a blender or food processor with the crème fraîche, horseradish, lemon zest and juice. Pulse until smooth. Season to taste with salt and pepper.

Serve the Yorkshire puddings, topped with the pea purée and rolled-up smoked salmon, with some lemon wedges for squeezing.

VARIATIONS
- If you don't have peas, just top with horseradish crème fraîche and dill.
- Use smoked trout instead of salmon.
- Serve with fine green beans or asparagus.
- Use cooked fresh peas instead of frozen.

YORKSHIRE PUDDING BURGERS

//

Mini Yorkshire puddings make a delicious alternative to burger buns – just sandwich the burgers between them and add your choice of garnishes and sauces.

SERVES 6
PREP 25 MINUTES
CHILL 20–30 MINUTES
COOK 20–25 MINUTES

500g (1lb 2oz/2¼ cups) lean minced (ground) beef
1 small red onion, grated
2 garlic cloves, crushed
1 medium free-range egg, beaten
12 tsp vegetable oil
salt and freshly ground black pepper
thinly sliced tomato, red onion and crisp lettuce, to serve
ketchup and/or mustard, for drizzling

BATTER
150g (5oz/1½ cups) plain (all-purpose) flour
¼ tsp salt
4 medium free-range eggs, beaten
360ml (12fl oz/1½ cups) milk

Preheat the oven to 220°C (200°C fan)/425°F/gas 7.

Make the burgers: mix the minced beef, onion, garlic and beaten egg together in a bowl. Season with salt and pepper, then divide the mixture into 6 equal-sized portions. Mould each one, with your hands, into a patty shape. Place on a plate, cover with cling film (plastic wrap) and chill in the fridge for 20–30 minutes to firm them up.

Make the batter: sift the flour and salt into a bowl. Beat in the eggs and a little milk. Gradually whisk in the remaining milk until you have a smooth batter. Transfer to a jug and set aside.

Put 1 teaspoon oil in each of the cups in a 12-hole muffin pan and place in the preheated oven for 5–10 minutes, until the oil is smoking and sizzling hot.

Quickly pour the batter into the cups and bake for 20–25 minutes, or until well-risen and golden brown. Do not open the oven door while the puddings are cooking or they may collapse.

Meanwhile, cook the burgers under a preheated grill (broiler) or in an oiled ridged griddle pan for about 5 minutes each side, or until cooked through to your liking.

Put some sliced tomato, onion and lettuce on 6 Yorkshires and top each one with a burger. Drizzle with ketchup and/or mustard and cover with the remaining Yorkshires. Eat immediately.

VARIATIONS
· Top the burger with a slice of cheese and flash under a hot grill (broiler) to melt it.
· Add some herbs or spices to the burger.
· Drizzle with hot sauce or add some relish.

YORKSHIRE PUDDING PIZZA WEDGES

Yorkshire pudding is so versatile that you can even use it as a pizza base. Try this tasty recipe and see for yourself. To make it really easy, we've used a bottled tomato pasta sauce for the topping.

SERVES 3–4
PREP 15 MINUTES
COOK 25–35 MINUTES

1 tbsp olive oil
175ml (6fl oz/¾ cup) Napoletana
   or other tomato pasta sauce
100g (4oz) mozzarella, sliced
rocket (arugula) or basil leaves,
   to garnish

BATTER
125g (4½oz/1¼ cups) plain
   (all-purpose) flour
¼ tsp salt
3 large free-range eggs, beaten
240ml (8fl oz/1 cup) milk

Preheat the oven to 220°C (200°C fan)/425°F/gas 7.

Make the batter: sift the flour and salt into a bowl. Beat in the eggs and a little milk. Gradually whisk in the remaining milk until you have a smooth batter without any lumps. Transfer to a jug and set aside.

Put the oil in a 25cm (10 inch) non-stick cake tin (pan) – use a springform pan if you have one to make turning out the pizza easier. Place in the preheated oven for 5–10 minutes, or until the oil is smoking and sizzling hot.

Quickly pour the batter into the tin and return to the oven immediately. Bake for 20–25 minutes, or until well-risen and golden brown. Do not open the oven door while the pudding is cooking or it may collapse.

Spoon the tomato sauce over the Yorkshire pudding and sprinkle the mozzarella over the top. Return to the oven for 5–10 minutes, or until the cheese melts and is bubbling.

Remove the pizza from the pan and sprinkle with rocket or basil leaves. Cut into wedges and serve immediately.

VARIATIONS
· Serve topped with thinly sliced prosciutto (Parma ham).
· Add some oregano, basil and black olives to the base tomato sauce.
· Add some artichoke hearts, sun-blush tomatoes or mushrooms.

YORKSHIRE PUDDING BURRITOS

//

To make these delicious burrito-style Yorkshires, you can either make the recipe on page 16 or four regular Yorkshire puddings (see below) and fold them over the filling. We've used traditional roast beef spiced with some hot sauce and guacamole to give it a Mexican flavour.

SERVES 4
PREP 20 MINUTES
COOK 20–25 MINUTES

Note: For the best results, you will need a non-stick deep 4-cup 23cm (9 inch) square Yorkshire pudding pan.

4 tsp vegetable oil
4 heaped tbsp guacamole
125g (4½oz) rare roast beef, thinly sliced or shredded
a few crisp lettuce leaves, shredded
3 tomatoes, cut into chunks
1 fresh or bottled jalapeño, chopped
a few sprigs of coriander (cilantro), chopped
salt and freshly ground black pepper
hot sauce, for drizzling

BATTER
125g (4½oz/1¼ cups) plain (all-purpose) flour
¼ tsp salt
3 large free-range eggs, beaten
240ml (8fl oz/1 cup) milk

Preheat the oven to 220°C (200°C fan)/425°F/gas 7.

Make the batter: sift the flour and salt into a bowl. Beat in the eggs and a little milk. Gradually whisk in the remaining milk until you have a smooth batter. Transfer to a jug and set aside.

Put 1 teaspoon oil in each of the 4 cups in the Yorkshire pudding pan and place in the preheated oven for 5–10 minutes, until the oil is smoking and sizzling hot.

Quickly pour the batter into the cups and return to the oven. Bake for 20–25 minutes, or until the batter rises and is well-risen and golden brown. Do not open the oven door while the puddings are cooking or they may collapse. Remove and leave to cool.

Flatten the Yorkshires by rolling them gently but firmly with a rolling pin. Spread each one with guacamole and top with the roast beef, lettuce, tomatoes, jalapeño and coriander. Season with salt and pepper, and drizzle with hot sauce.

Roll up the Yorkshires around the filling and secure by wrapping some kitchen foil around three-quarters of the length. Alternatively, secure with a cocktail stick (toothpick). Eat immediately.

VARIATIONS
· Add some soured cream or Greek yoghurt and salsa.
· Use leftover beef and cooked vegetables from the Sunday roast for the filling, then flavour with mustard or horseradish and serve drizzled with gravy.
· Use gherkins or dill pickles instead of chillies.
· Substitute roast chicken, turkey, lamb or pork for the beef.

ROAST VEGETABLE YORKSHIRE WRAPS

//

To make these wraps you'll need an ovenproof frying pan (skillet). Don't put one with a plastic or wooden handle in the hot oven, and be very careful when handling it – wear oven gloves!

SERVES 4
PREP 20 MINUTES
STAND 15 MINUTES
COOK 40 MINUTES

1 red onion, cut into 8 wedges
1 red (bell) pepper, deseeded and cut into chunks
1 green (bell) pepper, deseeded and cut into chunks
1 courgette (zucchini), thickly sliced
leaves stripped from 4 sprigs of thyme
4–5 tbsp olive oil
100g (4oz) feta cheese, crumbled
a few sprigs of parsley, chopped
salt and freshly ground black pepper
tzatziki, tahini sauce, pesto or hot sauce, to serve

BATTER
125g (4½oz/1¼ cups) plain (all-purpose) flour
¼ tsp salt
3 large free-range eggs, beaten
240ml (8fl oz/1 cup) milk

Preheat the oven to 220°C (200°C fan)/425°F/gas 7.

Make the batter: sift the flour and salt into a bowl. Beat in the eggs and a little milk. Gradually whisk in the remaining milk until you have a smooth batter. Transfer to a jug and stand for 15 minutes.

Put all the prepared vegetables in a roasting pan. Season with salt and pepper, sprinkle with thyme and drizzle with 3 tablespoons of the oil. Place on the middle or lower rack in the preheated oven and roast for 25–30 minutes, or until the vegetables are tender and starting to char. Remove and leave to cool a little.

Meanwhile, heat a 23cm (9 inch) ovenproof frying pan (skillet) on the highest rack in the oven until it's really hot. Remove and place on top of the hob over a high heat. Add 1 teaspoon of the oil and as soon as it starts to sizzle and smoke, quickly pour in one-quarter of the batter. Tilt the pan to swirl it around and cover the base evenly.

Place the pan at the top of the oven and bake for 5 minutes. Remove and carefully turn the Yorkshire wrap over. Pop back into the oven and cook for 5 minutes, or until puffy, set and golden brown. Slide out of the pan and place on a plate. Cover with foil and set aside to soften while you cook the other 3 wraps in the same way.

You can eat the wraps lukewarm or reheat them in a hot skillet or griddle pan when you are ready to assemble.

Divide the roasted vegetables among them and sprinkle with the feta and parsley. Fold the wraps over the filling or roll up and serve immediately with tzatziki, tahini sauce, pesto or hot sauce.

VARIATIONS
· Vary the vegetables: try aubergine (eggplant), tomatoes and mushrooms.

YORKSHIRE PUDDING TACOS

//

We've used homemade refried beans to fill these delicious vegetarian Yorkshire tacos, but you could use traditional chilli made with minced (ground) beef instead.

SERVES 4
PREP 25 MINUTES
COOK 20–25 MINUTES

Note: For the best results, you will need a non-stick deep 4-cup 23cm (9 inch) square Yorkshire pudding pan.

2 tbsp olive oil
1 onion, diced
2 garlic cloves, crushed
1 red chilli, diced
2 x 400g (14oz) tins red kidney
    beans, rinsed and drained
a small bunch of spring onions
    (scallions), diced
8 baby plum tomatoes, diced
a handful of coriander (cilantro),
    chopped
240g (8oz/1 cup) guacamole
100g (4oz/1 cup) grated Cheddar
    or Monterey Jack cheese
salt and freshly ground black
    pepper

BATTER
125g (4½oz/1¼ cups) plain
    (all-purpose) flour
¼ tsp salt
3 large free-range eggs, beaten
240ml (8fl oz/1 cup) milk

Preheat the oven to 220°C (200°C fan)/425°F/gas 7.

Make the batter: sift the flour and salt into a bowl. Beat in the eggs and a little milk. Gradually whisk in the remaining milk until you have a smooth batter. Transfer to a jug and set aside.

Put 1 teaspoon oil in each of the 4 cups in the Yorkshire pudding pan and place in the preheated oven for 5–10 minutes, until the oil is smoking and sizzling hot.

Quickly pour the batter into the cups and return to the oven immediately. Bake for 20–25 minutes, or until the batter rises and is well-risen and golden brown. Do not open the oven door while the puddings are cooking or they may collapse. Remove from the oven and leave to cool.

Meanwhile, heat the remaining oil in a frying pan (skillet) set over a medium heat and cook the onion, garlic and chilli, stirring occasionally, for 8–10 minutes, or until the onion is tender. Add the beans and heat through. Season to taste with salt and pepper.

Tip the mixture into a bowl and mash coarsely with a potato masher. Stir in the spring onions, tomatoes and most of the coriander.

Flatten the hot Yorkshires by rolling them gently but firmly with a rolling pin. Divide the hot bean mixture among them and top with the guacamole. Sprinkle with the remaining coriander and the grated cheese. Roll the Yorkshires around the filling and eat immediately.

VARIATIONS
· Serve with hot salsa and some soured cream.
· Use tinned refried beans instead of kidney beans.
· Add a dash of Tabasco to the bean filling mixture.

MAIN MEALS

CLASSIC TOAD IN THE HOLE

//

The secret to success is to make sure the oil or fat is smoking hot when you pour in the batter.
This will crisp up the base of the Yorkshire and you won't end up with a soggy pudding.

SERVES 4
PREP 10 MINUTES
STAND 30 MINUTES
COOK 35–45 MINUTES

1–2 tbsp vegetable oil or meat
    dripping
8 pork sausages
Onion Gravy, to serve
    (see page 23)
buttered cabbage or Brussels
    sprouts, to serve

BATTER
175g (6oz/1¾ cups) plain
    (all-purpose) flour
¼ tsp salt
4 large free-range eggs, beaten
420ml (14fl oz/1¾ cups) milk

Preheat the oven to 220°C (200°C fan)/425°F/gas 7.

Make the batter: sift the flour and salt into a bowl, then beat in
the eggs. Gradually beat in the milk, a little at a time, until you
have a smooth batter without lumps. Pour into a jug and set aside.

Put 1 tablespoon of the oil or dripping in a large roasting pan –
about 30 x 25cm (12 x 10 inch) – and place in the hot oven for
5–10 minutes, or until it is sizzling and smoking.

Add the sausages and cook in the oven for 5–7 minutes until
browned underneath. Turn them over and cook on the other side
for 5–7 minutes until browned. If there's not much fat in the pan
(the sausages will release more fat) add another tablespoon of
the oil or dripping.

Quickly pour in the batter and return the pan to the oven
immediately. Bake for 25–30 minutes, or until the batter is
well-risen, golden brown and crisp on top. Do not open the oven
door while the pudding is cooking or it may collapse.

Cut the Yorkshire into 4 pieces (each with 2 sausages) and serve
with Onion Gravy and buttered cabbage or Brussels sprouts.

VARIATIONS
- Add some chopped herbs or mustard to the Yorkshire
  batter.
- Use chipolatas (links) instead of fat sausages.
- Serve with mustard or horseradish.
- Use Quorn or plant-based sausages for a vegetarian
  toad in the hole.

LEFTOVER SUNDAY ROAST TOAD

//

This is real comfort food and a delicious way to use up leftover vegetables and stuffing from the Sunday roast. It's very versatile and you can adapt it to whatever you have available.

SERVES 4
PREP 15 MINUTES
STAND 30 MINUTES
COOK: 35–50 MINUTES

1–2 tbsp vegetable oil or meat dripping
4 sausages
4–6 leftover roast potatoes or parsnips, cut into large chunks
4 leftover stuffing balls (see page 43) or large spoonfuls of stuffing
150g (5oz) leftover Brussels sprouts and/or carrots
cranberry sauce and gravy (see pages 23–25), to serve

BATTER
175g (6oz/1¾ cups) plain (all-purpose) flour
¼ tsp salt
4 large free-range eggs, beaten
420ml (14fl oz/1¾ cups) milk

Preheat the oven to 220°C (200°C fan)/425°F/gas 7.

Make the batter: sift the flour and salt into a bowl, then beat in the eggs. Gradually beat in the milk, a little at a time, until you have a smooth batter without lumps. Pour into a jug and set aside.

Put 1 tablespoon of the oil or dripping in a large roasting pan – about 30 x 25cm (12 x 10 inch) – and place in the hot oven for 5–10 minutes, or until it is sizzling and smoking.

Add the sausages and cook in the oven for 5–7 minutes until browned underneath. Turn them over and add the potatoes or parsnips and the stuffing balls plus more oil or dripping if needed. Return the pan to the oven and cook for about 5–10 minutes, or until browned.

Quickly pour in the batter and add the sprouts and/or carrots. Return the pan to the oven immediately and bake for about 25–30 minutes, or until the batter is well-risen, golden brown and crisp on top. Do not open the oven door while the pudding is cooking or it may collapse.

Cut the Yorkshire into 4 pieces (each with a sausage, some stuffing, potatoes or parsnips and vegetables) and serve immediately with cranberry sauce and gravy.

VARIATIONS
· Serve with apple jelly, horseradish or mustard.
· Add some bacon-wrapped prunes or leftover bacon-wrapped chipolatas (links).
· Add some leftover leeks, broccoli or cauliflower florets.

BUTTERNUT SQUASH AND BLUE CHEESE TOAD

//

The addition of blue cheese to this vegetarian toad in the hole is what makes it so delicious. Creamy Gorgonzola, Dolcelatte or Cambozola work best, but you could substitute crumbled Roquefort or even Stilton.

SERVES 4
PREP 20 MINUTES
STAND 30 MINUTES
COOK 50–60 MINUTES

1 small butternut squash, peeled, deseeded and cubed
2 red onions, sliced
2 garlic cloves, crushed
leaves stripped from 3 sprigs of thyme
3 tbsp olive oil
150g (5oz) blue cheese, e.g. Gorgonzola, diced
salt and freshly ground black pepper
red onion marmalade or redcurrant jelly, to serve

BATTER
175g (6oz/1¾ cups) plain (all-purpose) flour
¼ tsp salt
4 large free-range eggs, beaten
420ml (14fl oz/1¾ cups) milk
a few sprigs of parsley, chopped

Preheat the oven to 200°C (180°C fan)/400°F/gas 6.

Make the batter: sift the flour and salt into a bowl, then beat in the eggs. Gradually beat in the milk, a little at a time, until you have a smooth batter without any lumps. Stir in the parsley, pour into a jug and set aside.

Put the squash, onion and garlic in a large roasting pan – about 30 x 25cm (12 x 10 inch). Scatter the thyme over the top and drizzle with the oil. Season lightly with salt and pepper and cook in the oven for 25–30 minutes, or until the vegetables are tender.

Turn up the oven to 220°C (200°C fan)/425°F/gas 7. Remove the pan from the oven and scatter the blue cheese over the top.

When the temperature is reached, quickly pour in the batter and return the pan to the oven immediately. Bake for 25–30 minutes, or until well-risen, golden brown and crisp on top. Do not open the oven door while the pudding is cooking or it may collapse.

Cut the toad into 4 slabs and serve with red onion marmalade or redcurrant jelly.

VARIATIONS
· Use sweet potato or pumpkin instead of squash.
· Substitute a different cheese, e.g. goat's cheese, Brie or feta.

SPANISH CHORIZO AND RED PEPPER TOAD

///

Make your toad in the hole extra special by giving it a Spanish twist. We've added chorizo, red peppers, smoked paprika and garlic for all you spice lovers.

SERVES 4
PREP 20 MINUTES
COOK 35–40 MINUTES

250g (9oz) chorizo, cut into
   chunks (or 12 mini chorizo
   sausages)
1 red onion, cut into 8 wedges
2 red (bell) peppers, deseeded
   and cut into chunks
2 tbsp vegetable oil
salt and freshly ground black
   pepper
green vegetables, to serve

BATTER
175g (6oz/1¾ cups) plain
   (all-purpose) flour
1 tsp smoked paprika
¼ tsp salt
4 large free-range eggs, beaten
420ml (14fl oz/1¾ cups) milk
3 garlic cloves, crushed

Preheat the oven to 220°C (200°C fan)/425°F/gas 7.

Make the batter: sift the flour, smoked paprika and salt into a bowl, then beat in the eggs. Gradually beat in the milk, a little at a time, until you have a smooth batter without any lumps. Stir in the garlic, pour into a jug and set aside.

Put the chorizo, onions and red pepper in a large roasting pan – about 30 x 25cm (12 x 10 inch). Drizzle with the oil and season lightly with salt and pepper. Cook in the oven for 10 minutes, turning the chorizo once.

Quickly pour in the batter and pop the pan back into the oven immediately. Bake for 25–30 minutes, or until well-risen, golden brown and crisp on top. Do not open the oven door while the pudding is cooking or it may collapse.

Cut into 4 slabs and serve immediately with some green vegetables.

VARIATIONS
· Add some ground chilli or crushed dried chilli flakes
   to the batter.
· Serve with Roasted Red Onion and Wine Gravy
   (see page 25).
· Substitute sherry or Madeira for the wine in the gravy.

YORKSHIRE PUDDING WITH RAGU

//

This is great comfort food – perfect for a cold winter's day. You could make double the quantity of ragu and freeze one portion or serve it with pasta for supper on another evening.

SERVES 4
PREP 20 MINUTES
STAND 15 MINUTES
COOK 1 HOUR

Note: You will need a non-stick deep 4-cup 23cm (9 inch) square Yorkshire pudding pan.

2 tbsp olive oil
1 onion, finely chopped
2 garlic cloves, crushed
2 carrots, diced
2 celery sticks, diced
400g (14oz/1¾ cups) minced (ground) lean beef
240ml (8fl oz/1 cup) milk
a pinch of ground nutmeg
240ml (8fl oz/1 cup) red or white wine
1 x 400g (14oz) tin chopped tomatoes
2 tbsp tomato purée
a good pinch of dried oregano or marjoram
4 tsp vegetable oil
salt and freshly ground black pepper
green vegetables, to serve

BATTER

125g (4½oz/1¼ cups) plain (all-purpose) flour
¼ tsp salt
3 large free-range eggs, beaten
240ml (8fl oz/1 cup) milk

Make the batter: sift the flour and salt into a bowl. Beat in the eggs and a little milk. Gradually whisk in the remaining milk until you have a smooth batter without any lumps. Transfer to a jug and set aside.

Heat the olive oil in a saucepan set over a medium heat. Cook the onion, garlic, carrot and celery, stirring occasionally, for 5 minutes, or until starting to soften. Add the minced beef and cook, stirring occasionally, for 5 minutes, or until browned.

Reduce the heat to low and stir in the milk and nutmeg. Cook for 20 minutes, or until the milk evaporates. Stir in the wine, tomatoes, tomato purée and herbs, and cook gently for 30 minutes, or until the sauce has thickened. Season to taste.

Preheat the oven to 220°C (200°C fan)/425°F/gas 7.

When the oven is hot, put 1 teaspoon vegetable oil in each of the 4 cups in the Yorkshire pudding pan and place in the oven for 5–10 minutes, or until the oil is smoking and sizzling hot.

Quickly pour the batter into the cups and return to the oven immediately. Bake for 20–25 minutes, or until well-risen and golden brown. Do not open the oven door while the pudding is cooking or it may collapse.

Turn the puddings out of the pan and serve immediately filled with the ragu sauce, with some green vegetables on the side.

VARIATIONS
· Spoon the ragu sauce into a hot baking dish and pour the Yorkshire batter over the top. Bake for 20–25 minutes.

GARLICKY SHRIMP IN THE HOLE

///

If you love the garlic and lemon flavours of shrimp scampi, why not try adding the same ingredients to Yorkshire pudding? It's so simple and delicious. You can buy frozen raw prawns (shrimp) in most supermarkets and fishmongers. Defrost them thoroughly in the fridge before cooking them.

SERVES 4
PREP 15 MINUTES
COOK 40–45 MINUTES

2 tbsp olive oil
30g (1oz/2 tbsp) unsalted butter
4 spring onions (scallions),
   thinly sliced
5 garlic cloves, crushed
juice of 1 small lemon
4 tbsp white wine
450g (1lb) raw prawns (shrimp),
   shelled and deveined
a handful of parsley, chopped
salt and freshly ground
   black pepper
green vegetables, to serve

BATTER
175g (6oz/1¾ cups) plain
   (all-purpose) flour
1 tsp smoked paprika
¼ tsp salt
4 large free-range eggs, beaten
420ml (14fl oz/1¾ cups) milk

Preheat the oven to 220°C (200°C fan)/425°F/gas 7.

Make the batter: sift the flour, smoked paprika and salt into a bowl, then beat in the eggs. Gradually beat in the milk, a little at a time, until you have a smooth batter without any lumps. Pour the batter into a jug and set aside.

Put the olive oil and butter in a large roasting pan (or large ovenproof frying pan) that you can use on the hob. Set over a medium heat and cook the spring onions and garlic for 3–4 minutes until softened but not coloured. Stir in the lemon juice and wine and let it bubble away for 5 minutes until the liquid reduces.

Add the prawns in a single layer and cook for 2–3 minutes until pink underneath. Turn them over and cook the other side until pink. Stir in the parsley and season to taste.

Quickly pour in the batter and place immediately near the top of the preheated oven. Bake for 25–30 minutes, or until well-risen, golden brown and crisp on top. Do not open the oven door while the pudding is cooking or it may collapse.

Cut into 4 slabs and serve immediately with green vegetables.

VARIATIONS
• Add some dried red pepper flakes.
• Substitute chives or coriander (cilantro) for the parsley.
• Use white vermouth instead of white wine.

COTTAGE PIE YORKIES

//

Cottage pie and Yorkshire pudding are both traditional British dishes, but we've combined these family favourites to create some real comfort food. You can cook the Yorkshires fresh or heat up some ready-made ones for this hearty supper.

SERVES 6
PREP 25 MINUTES
COOK 45–60 MINUTES

12 Individual Yorkshire Puddings (see page 16)
2 tbsp olive oil
1 large onion, finely chopped
2 celery sticks, chopped
2 large carrots, chopped
450g (1lb/2 cups) lean minced (ground) beef
240ml (8fl oz/1 cup) hot beef stock
2 tbsp tomato purée
a dash of Worcestershire sauce
1 tbsp cornflour (cornstarch)
4 large baking potatoes, peeled and cut into chunks
25g (1oz/2 tbsp) butter
3 tbsp milk
100g (4oz/1 cup) grated Cheddar cheese
salt and freshly ground black pepper
buttered cabbage or Brussels sprouts, to serve

If you're making the Yorkshires from scratch, preheat the oven, make the batter and cook them as per the recipe on page 16.

Meanwhile, heat the oil in a saucepan set over a medium heat. Cook the onion, celery and carrot, stirring occasionally, for 5 minutes, or until softened. Stir in the minced beef and cook for 5–10 minutes until browned all over.

Add the beef stock, tomato purée and Worcestershire sauce. Season with salt and pepper. Reduce the heat and simmer for 20 minutes, or until the sauce has reduced. Mix the cornflour in a small basin with a little water to make a smooth paste and stir into the minced beef mixture to thicken the sauce.

Meanwhile, cook the potatoes in a pan of boiling salted water for 10–15 minutes until tender. Drain well and mash with the butter and milk. Season to taste.

Preheat the oven to 200°C (180°C fan)/400°F/gas 6 if you aren't cooking the Yorkshires fresh.

Divide the minced beef mixture among the hot Yorkshire puddings – if you made them in advance, reheat them in a muffin pan or on a baking tray. Put a heaped spoonful of mashed potato on top of each one and sprinkle with the grated Cheddar.

Cook the Yorkshires in the oven for 5–10 minutes, or until the cheese melts and the filling is really hot. Serve immediately with buttered cabbage or Brussels sprouts.

VARIATIONS
• Use minced lamb or Quorn instead of beef.

IRISH TOAD IN THE HOLE

Adding Guinness to the Yorkshire batter gives it more flavour and a special Irish touch.
For a really warming supper, serve it with lashings of gravy and buttered seasonal green vegetables.

SERVES 4
PREP 15 MINUTES
COOK 40–50 MINUTES

2 tbsp vegetable oil or meat dripping
8 pork sausages
2 onions, thinly sliced
4 thick slices of black pudding, skinned and halved
a handful of parsley, chopped
Onion Gravy, to serve (see page 23)
green vegetables, e.g. kale, cabbage or sprouts, to serve

BATTER
175g (6oz/1¾ cups) plain (all-purpose) flour
¼ tsp salt
4 large free-range eggs, beaten
240ml (8fl oz/1 cup) milk
180ml (6fl oz/¾ cup) Guinness or stout
1 tbsp wholegrain mustard

Preheat the oven to 220°C (200°C fan)/425°F/gas 7.

Make the batter: sift the flour and salt into a bowl, then make a well in the centre and beat in the eggs. Gradually beat in the milk and Guinness (or stout) until you have a smooth batter without lumps. Stir in the mustard and then pour into a jug and set aside.

Put 1 tablespoon of the oil or dripping in a large roasting pan – about 30 x 25cm (12 x 10 inch) – and place in the hot oven for 5 minutes. Add the sausages, onion and black pudding and cook in the oven for 5–7 minutes until browned underneath. Turn them over and cook on the other side for 5–7 minutes.

Remove from the pan and set aside. Add the remaining oil to the pan and pop it back into the oven for 5–10 minutes, or until it is sizzling and smoking.

Quickly return the sausages, onion and black pudding to the pan. Sprinkle with parsley and pour in the batter. Bake in the oven for 25–30 minutes, or until well-risen, golden brown and crisp. Do not open the oven door while it is cooking or it may collapse.

Cut the toad into 4 pieces (each with 2 sausages and some black pudding) and serve with Onion Gravy and green vegetables.

VARIATIONS
· Use sliced chorizo instead of black pudding.
· Use red onions and vary the herbs.

ITALIAN-STYLE ROASTED VEGETABLE YORKSHIRE

//

In Italy, a dish of roasted vegetables is called *pasticcio*, which literally means 'a mess'. You can throw in virtually any vegetables you have in the fridge and this will still taste good. Cavolo nero is a Tuscan cabbage that is so dark in colour that it's almost black. You can buy it in many supermarkets and farmers' markets or use kale as a substitute.

SERVES 4
PREP 20 MINUTES
COOK 50–60 MINUTES

1 fat fennel bulb, trimmed
    and cut into slices
1 large onion, cut into wedges
4 Portobello mushrooms,
    quartered
a few sprigs of rosemary and
    thyme
4 tbsp olive oil
a large handful of cavolo nero,
    sliced
salt and freshly ground black
    pepper
Mushroom Gravy (see page 24),
    to serve

BATTER
175g (6oz/1¾ cups) plain
    (all-purpose) flour
¼ tsp salt
4 large free-range eggs, beaten
420ml (14fl oz/1¾ cups) milk
2 garlic cloves, crushed

Preheat the oven to 200°C (180°C fan)/400°F/gas 6.

Place the fennel, onion and Portobello mushrooms in a large roasting pan. Add the herbs and drizzle with 3 tablespoons of the oil. Season lightly with salt and pepper. Roast in the oven for 15 minutes, then turn the vegetables over. Return to the oven and roast for a further 10–15 minutes, or until they are cooked and tender.

Meanwhile, make the batter: sift the flour and salt into a bowl, then make a well in the centre and beat in the eggs. Gradually beat in the milk until you have a smooth batter without any lumps. Stir in the garlic, then pour into a jug and leave to stand.

When the vegetables are cooked, remove from the pan and set aside, discarding the herbs. Add the remaining oil to the pan and increase the oven temperature to 220°C (200°C fan)/425°F/gas 7. Return the pan to the oven for 5–10 minutes, or until the oil is really hot and starting to smoke.

Quickly put the cavolo nero and roasted vegetables in the pan. Pour in the batter and cook in the oven for 25–30 minutes or until well-risen, golden brown and crisp on top. Do not open the oven door while the pudding is cooking or it may collapse.

Cut into 4 portions and serve immediately with Mushroom Gravy.

VARIATIONS
- Add some sliced celeriac or celery.
- Substitute spring greens or kale for the cavolo nero.
- Add some diced Taleggio or Gorgonzola when you add the batter to the pan.

HERBY HADDOCK YORKSHIRE PUFFS

//

If you've never thought of adding fish to a Yorkshire pudding batter, now's the time to try. These tasty little puffs make a delightful change to fish and chips. And the tartare sauce is so quick and easy to make. You can prepare it the day before and cover and chill in the fridge overnight.

SERVES 4–6
PREP 15 MINUTES
COOK 20–25 MINUTES

12 tsp vegetable oil
green beans, peas or broccoli,
   to serve
lemon wedges, for squeezing

BATTER
250g (9oz/2½ cups) plain
   (all-purpose) flour
¼ tsp salt
4 large free-range eggs, beaten
300ml (½ pint/1¼ cups) milk
a small handful of dill, chopped
400g (14oz) skinned smoked
   haddock fillets, cubed

TARTARE SAUCE
200ml (7fl oz/scant 1 cup)
   mayonnaise
2 tbsp capers, rinsed, drained
   and chopped
5 cornichons (mini gherkins),
   drained and chopped
3 spring onions (scallions),
   thinly sliced
a few sprigs of parsley, chopped
a good squeeze of lemon juice
salt and freshly ground black
   pepper

Preheat the oven to 220°C (200°C fan)/425°F/gas 7.

Make the batter: sift the flour and salt into a bowl. Beat in the eggs and a little milk. Gradually whisk in the remaining milk until you have a smooth batter without any lumps. Stir in the dill and smoked haddock.

Put 1 teaspoon oil in each of the cups in a deep 12-hole muffin pan and place in the preheated oven for 5–10 minutes, or until the oil is smoking and sizzling hot.

Quickly ladle the batter into the cups, distributing the haddock evenly among them, and bake in the oven for 20–25 minutes, or until well-risen and golden brown. Do not open the oven door while the puddings are cooking or they may collapse.

Meanwhile, make the tartare sauce: mix all the ingredients together in a bowl and season to taste.

Turn out the Yorkshires and serve immediately with the tartare sauce, some green vegetables and lemon wedges for squeezing.

VARIATIONS
· Use smoked cod, mackerel or trout instead of haddock.
· Use a 50:50 mixture of haddock and tiny shelled prawns (shrimp).
· Substitute parsley for the dill.

CHILLI YORKSHIRES

//

These individual Yorkshire puddings are filled with delicious vegetarian black bean chilli.

SERVES 4
PREP 20 MINUTES
COOK 20–25 MINUTES

Note: You will need a non-stick deep 4-cup 23cm (9 inch) square Yorkshire pudding pan.

4 tsp vegetable oil
2 tbsp olive oil
1 large onion, finely chopped
2 garlic cloves, crushed
1 red (bell) pepper, deseeded and chopped
1–2 tsp chilli powder
1 x 400g (14oz) tin chopped tomatoes
2 tbsp tomato purée
1 x 400g (14oz) tin black beans, rinsed and drained
a few sprigs of coriander (cilantro), chopped
salt and freshly ground black pepper
diced avocado and soured cream, to serve

BATTER
125g (4½oz/1¼ cups) plain (all-purpose) flour
¼ tsp salt
3 large free-range eggs, beaten
240ml (8fl oz/1 cup) milk

Preheat the oven to 220°C (200°C fan)/425°F/gas 7.

Make the batter: sift the flour and salt into a bowl. Beat in the eggs and a little milk. Gradually whisk in the remaining milk until you have a smooth batter without any lumps. Transfer to a jug and set aside.

Put 1 teaspoon vegetable oil in each of the 4 cups in the Yorkshire pudding pan and place in the preheated oven for 5–10 minutes, until the oil is smoking and sizzling hot.

Quickly pour the batter into the cups and place in the oven immediately. Bake for 20–25 minutes, or until well-risen and golden brown. Do not open the oven door while the puddings are cooking or they may collapse.

Meanwhile, heat the olive oil in a pan set over a low to medium heat. Cook the onion, garlic and red pepper, stirring occasionally, for 6–8 minutes until tender. Stir in the chilli powder and cook for 1 minute. Add the tomatoes, tomato purée and beans and simmer gently for 10–15 minutes, or until the mixture reduces and thickens. Stir in the coriander and season to taste.

Turn the Yorkshires out of the pan and place on 4 serving plates. Divide the chilli among them and top with some avocado and soured cream. Serve immediately.

VARIATIONS
· Use red kidney beans instead of black beans.
· Add a diced fresh chilli or bottled jalapeños.
· Sprinkle some grated Cheddar cheese over the chilli before serving.
· Add some minced (ground) beef to the chilli.

ROASTED VEGETABLE YORKSHIRE TRAY BAKE

This recipe is so versatile and you can adapt it easily to the vegetables you have available in your fridge or larder. Instead of gravy, serve it with a creamy homemade mushroom sauce or drizzled with fresh pesto.

SERVES 4
PREP 20 MINUTES
COOK 40–45 MINUTES

2 leeks, thinly sliced
1 large red onion, thinly sliced
4 Portobello mushrooms
3 tbsp olive oil
4 sprigs of cherry tomatoes on the vine
crisp salad or green vegetables, to serve

BATTER
175g (6oz/1¾ cups) plain (all-purpose) flour
¼ tsp salt
a pinch of ground nutmeg
4 large free-range eggs, beaten
420ml (14fl oz/1¾ cups) milk
a small handful of parsley, chopped

Preheat the oven to 220°C (200°C fan)/425°F/gas 7.

Make the batter: sift the flour, salt and nutmeg into a bowl, then beat in the eggs. Gradually beat in the milk, a little at a time, until you have a smooth batter without any lumps. Stir in the parsley, pour the batter into a jug and set aside.

Put the leeks, onion and mushrooms, open-side down, in a large roasting pan. Drizzle with the oil and cook in the preheated oven for 10 minutes. Turn the mushrooms over and cook for 5 minutes more.

Quickly pour the batter over the vegetables and place the tomatoes on the vine on top. Return to the oven immediately and cook for 25–30 minutes or until the batter is well-risen, crisp on top and golden brown. Do not open the oven door while the pudding is cooking or it may collapse.

Serve immediately, cut into wedges, with a crisp salad or some green vegetables.

VARIATIONS
- Add some asparagus spears, shelled peas or some shredded spinach leaves.
- Add some drained artichoke hearts.
- Use chestnut mushrooms instead of Portobello ones.
- Stir some grated cheese into the batter.

SNACKS

SMOKED SALMON YORKSHIRE 'BLINIS'

///

Mini Yorkshires make wonderful snacks and party canapés. Crisp on the outside but soft in the middle, they are the perfect base for a variety of delicious toppings. All you need is a mini muffin pan.

MAKES 12
PREP 20 MINUTES
STAND 15 MINUTES
COOK 10–12 MINUTES

2 tbsp vegetable oil
100ml (4fl oz/⅓ cup) soured
    cream or crème fraîche
2 tsp horseradish sauce
100g (4oz) smoked salmon, diced
juice of ½ lemon
a few chives, snipped
freshly ground black pepper

BATTER
50g (2oz/generous ½ cup) plain
    (all-purpose) flour
¼ tsp salt
1 large free-range egg, beaten
60ml (2fl oz/¼ cup) milk

Preheat the oven to 220°C (200°C fan)/425°F/gas 7.

Make the batter: sift the flour into a bowl with the salt. Add the beaten egg with a little of the milk and whisk until combined. Gradually beat in the rest of the milk until you have a smooth batter without any lumps. Transfer to a jug and set aside to stand for 15 minutes.

Put a little oil in each cup of a 12-hole mini muffin pan. Place on a high shelf in the hot oven for 5–10 minutes, or until the fat is hissing, sizzling and smoking.

Quickly pour the batter into the cups (about halfway up each one) and place in the oven. Cook for 10–12 minutes, or until the mini Yorkshires are well-risen, crisp and golden brown. Do not open the oven door while the puddings are cooking or they may collapse. Place on a wire rack and leave until cool.

Put the mini Yorkshires on a serving platter. Mix the soured cream or crème fraîche with the horseradish and top each mini Yorkshire with a heaped teaspoonful.

Sprinkle the smoked salmon with lemon juice and pile on top of the Yorkshires. Add some pepper and a sprinkle of chives to serve.

VARIATIONS
- Use cream cheese instead of soured cream or crème fraîche.
- Use dill instead of chives.
- Substitute caviar, lumpfish roe or diced prawns (shrimp) for the smoked salmon.
- Or top with a strip of rare roast beef and a cornichon (mini gherkin).

CHEESY RED ONION CHUTNEY YORKSHIRE BITES

//

These cheesy mini Yorkshires are great eaten as snacks or party nibbles, or served with pre-dinner drinks. If you're in a hurry, you can use bought frozen Yorkshire puddings. These tend to be larger so you may have to double the quantities of cheese and chutney before baking in the hot oven for 8–10 minutes.

MAKES 12
PREP 15 MINUTES
STAND 15 MINUTES
COOK 13–16 MINUTES

2 tbsp vegetable oil
75g (3oz) goat's cheese
12 tsp red onion chutney

BATTER
50g (2oz/generous ½ cup) plain
    (all-purpose) flour
¼ tsp salt
1 large free-range egg, beaten
60ml (2fl oz/¼ cup) milk

Preheat the oven to 220°C (200°C fan)/425°F/gas 7.

Make the batter: sift the flour into a bowl with the salt. Add the beaten egg with a little of the milk and whisk until combined. Gradually beat in the rest of the milk until you have a smooth batter without any lumps. Transfer to a jug and set aside to stand for 15 minutes.

Put a little oil in each cup of a 12-hole mini muffin pan. Place on a high shelf in the hot oven for 5–10 minutes, or until the fat is hissing, sizzling and smoking.

Quickly pour the batter into the cups (about halfway up each one) and cook for 10–12 minutes, or until well-risen, crisp and golden brown. Do not open the oven door while the puddings are cooking or they may collapse.

Remove from the oven and crumble some goat's cheese into the hollow in the top of each Yorkshire pudding and top with a spoonful of red onion chutney. Pop back into the oven for about 3–4 minutes to warm the filling and make the Yorkshires even crispier and browner. Serve hot or lukewarm.

VARIATIONS
• Use grated Cheddar instead of goat's cheese.
• Top with spicy mango or peach chutney.

BRIE AND CRANBERRY YORKSHIRE NIBBLES

These mini Yorkshires taste great at any time of the year but they come into their own at Christmas, when you can serve them as festive party canapés.

MAKES 12
PREP 15 MINUTES
STAND 15 MINUTES
COOK 10–12 MINUTES

2 tbsp vegetable oil
75g (3oz) firm Brie, cut into
    12 small cubes
12 level tsp cranberry sauce,
    plus extra to serve

BATTER
50g (2oz/generous ½ cup) plain
    (all-purpose) flour
¼ tsp salt
1 large free-range egg, beaten
60ml (2fl oz/¼ cup) milk

Preheat the oven to 220°C (200°C fan)/425°F/gas 7.

Make the batter: sift the flour into a bowl with the salt. Add the beaten egg with a little of the milk and whisk until combined. Gradually beat in the rest of the milk until you have a smooth batter without any lumps. Transfer to a jug and set aside to stand for 15 minutes.

Put a little oil in each cup of a 12-hole mini muffin pan. Place on a high shelf in the hot oven for 5–10 minutes, or until the fat is hissing, sizzling and smoking.

Quickly pour the batter into the cups (about halfway up each one). Add a cube of Brie and a level teaspoon of cranberry sauce to each one. Cook for 10–12 minutes, or until well-risen, crisp and golden brown. Do not open the oven door while the puddings are cooking or they may collapse.

Serve hot or lukewarm drizzled with a little cranberry sauce.

VARIATIONS
· Use fruity chutney or quince paste instead of the cranberry sauce.
· Use apple sauce and cubes of Camembert.
· Serve sprinkled with chives or parsley.

YORKSHIRE PUDDING NACHOS

///

Yorkshire puddings are a great way of serving nachos. Not only do they taste delicious but they are less messy and easier to eat. We've used 12 individual mini Yorkshires, but you could make the puddings in a shallow 4-hole Yorkshire pudding pan instead if serving them as a main course.

MAKES 12
PREP 10 MINUTES
COOK 10–12 MINUTES

12 Individual Yorkshire Puddings
    (see page 16)
100g (4oz) tortilla chips
12 baby plum or cherry tomatoes,
    quartered
1 x 200g (7oz) tin red kidney
    beans, rinsed and drained
6 spring onions (scallions), thinly
    sliced
1 red or green chilli, diced
a small handful of coriander
    (cilantro), chopped
150g (5oz/1 cup) salsa or pico
    de gallo
100g (4oz/1 cup) grated
    Cheddar cheese
guacamole and soured cream,
    to serve (optional)

If you're making the Yorkshires from scratch, preheat the oven, make the batter and cook them as per the recipe on page 16.

When they are cooked or if you aren't cooking the Yorkshires fresh, adjust the heat to 200°C (180°C fan)/400°F/gas 6.

Coarsely crumble the tortilla chips (break each one into 2–3 pieces) and place in a bowl with the tomatoes, beans, spring onions, chilli and coriander. Stir in the salsa or pico de gallo.

Place the Yorkshire puddings on a baking sheet and divide the mixture among them. Sprinkle with the grated cheese.

Bake in the preheated oven for 10–12 minutes, or until the cheese melts and the Yorkshires are hot and crispy.

Serve immediately with guacamole and soured cream (if using).

VARIATIONS
· Use black beans instead of kidney beans.
· Add some sweetcorn kernels.
· Add some diced avocado tossed in lime juice.
· For extra heat, add more chilli or a dash of hot sauce.

SPICY JAMAICAN POPOVERS

Fresh and hot from the oven, these spicy popovers are a real treat. Don't worry if you have some left over – just reheat in a preheated oven at 180°C (160°C fan)/350°F/gas 4 for 5–10 minutes and they will crisp up nicely.

MAKES 6–10
PREP 10 MINUTES
COOK 30 MINUTES

Note: If you don't have a 6-hole popover pan just use a standard 12-hole muffin pan in which case the quantities given will make approximately 9–10 popovers.

125g (4oz/1¼ cups) plain
   (all-purpose) flour
½ tsp salt
1 tsp freshly ground black pepper
1 tsp freshly grated nutmeg
a pinch of ground allspice
3 large free-range eggs
240ml (8fl oz/1 cup) milk
5 tbsp melted butter

Preheat the oven to 220°C (200°C fan)/425°F/gas 7.

Make the batter: sift the flour into a bowl and stir in the salt, black pepper, nutmeg and allspice. Beat together the eggs, milk and 2 tablespoons of the melted butter with a balloon whisk or hand-held electric whisk. Gradually add the liquid mixture to the flour, stirring all the time, until you have a smooth batter without any lumps. Transfer to a jug and set aside.

Put a little melted butter in each cup of a 6-hole straight-sided popover pan or a 12-cup muffin pan. Place in the hot oven for 5 minutes, or until the butter starts to sizzle.

Quickly pour the batter into the cups (about halfway up) and bake for 15 minutes. Reduce the heat to 180°C (160°C fan)/350°F/gas 4 and bake for a further 15 minutes, without opening the oven door, or until the popovers are crisp, puffed up and golden brown. Do not open the oven door while the popovers are cooking or they may collapse.

Remove the popovers from the pan and, to enjoy them at their best, eat them piping hot.

VARIATIONS
· Try other spices – smoked paprika, ground cumin, cinnamon and cayenne.
· Add some red pepper flakes or crushed dried chilli flakes.
· Add some dried herbs – thyme, oregano or marjoram.

TAKOYAKI

//

If you like Japanese flavours, seafood and Yorkshires, you'll love these little beauties, which are traditionally made with diced octopus or squid and sold as street food. Crisp on the outside and soft in the centre, takoyaki have the perfect umami flavour. They are usually round and made in a special pan, but we have used a mini muffin pan instead and they still taste delicious.

MAKES 12
PREP 15 MINUTES
COOK 10–15 MINUTES

420ml (14fl oz/1¾ cups) dashi stock (made with dashi powder)
1 tsp soy sauce, plus extra for drizzling
3 large free-range eggs, beaten
125g (4½ oz/1¼ cups) plain (all-purpose) flour, plus extra for dusting
2 tsp baking powder
½ tsp salt
175g (6oz) cooked squid or octopus, diced
4 spring onions (scallions), thinly sliced
12 tsp vegetable oil, plus extra for brushing
2 tbsp red pickled ginger, chopped
chopped red chilli, to garnish (optional)

Preheat the oven to 220°C (200°C fan)/425°F/gas 7.

Make up the dashi according to the instructions on the packet.

In a bowl, whisk the dashi with the soy sauce and beaten eggs. Add the flour, baking powder and salt and whisk until well blended and you have a smooth batter without any lumps.

Lightly dust the squid or octopus with flour and stir into the batter with the spring onions. Transfer the batter to a jug.

Brush each cup of a 12-hole muffin pan with oil and then pour in an extra teaspoonful to a depth of 1mm. Place in the hot oven for 5–10 minutes, or until the oil starts to sizzle and smoke.

Quickly pour the batter into the cups and sprinkle with the pickled ginger. Bake in the preheated oven for 5 minutes, or until the batter is set and brown underneath. Gently flip the takoyaki over and bake for 5–10 minutes, or until they are crisp, puffed up and golden brown all over.

Remove from the pan and eat them piping hot, drizzled with soy sauce and garnished with red chilli if liked.

VARIATIONS
· Use diced prawns (shrimp) instead of squid or octopus.
· Vegetarians can substitute shiitake mushrooms.
· Sprinkle the cooked takoyaki with nori flakes or bonito flakes.
· Serve with Japanese mayonnaise or takoyaki sauce.
· Sprinkle with ponzu.

PARMESAN LEMON POPOVERS

///

The lemon zest gives these Parmesan popovers a bit of a flavour kick. They taste best eaten hot and fresh from the oven.

MAKES 6–10
PREP 10 MINUTES
COOK 30 MINUTES

Note: If you don't have a 6-hole popover pan just use a standard 12-hole muffin pan in which case the quantities given will make approximately 9–10 popovers.

125g (4oz/1¼ cups) plain (all-purpose) flour
½ tsp salt
a pinch of freshly ground black pepper
a pinch of freshly grated nutmeg
3 large free-range eggs
240ml (8fl oz/1 cup) milk
5 tbsp melted butter
25g (1oz/¼ cup) grated Parmesan cheese
grated zest of 1 large unwaxed lemon
1 tbsp thyme leaves

Preheat the oven to 220°C (200°C fan)/425°F/gas 7.

Make the batter: sift the flour into a bowl and stir in the salt, pepper and nutmeg. Beat together the eggs, milk and 2 tablespoons of the melted butter with a balloon whisk or hand-held electric whisk. Gradually add the liquid mixture to the flour, beating all the time, until you have a smooth batter without any lumps. Stir in the Parmesan, lemon zest and thyme.

Put a little melted butter in each cup of a 6-cup straight-sided popover pan or a 12-cup muffin pan. Place in the hot oven for 5 minutes, or until the butter starts to sizzle.

Quickly pour the batter into the cups (about halfway up) and bake for 15 minutes. Reduce the heat to 180°C (160°C fan)/350°F/gas 4 and bake for a further 15 minutes, or until the popovers are crisp, puffed up and golden brown. Do not open the oven door while the popovers are cooking or they may collapse.

Remove the popovers from the pan and, to enjoy them at their best, eat them piping hot.

VARIATIONS
· Add some crumbled crispy bacon or pancetta.
· Vary the herbs: try chives or parsley.
· Sprinkle the popovers with more grated Parmesan.

JALAPEÑO CHEDDAR POPOVERS

//

These delicious cheesy popovers make a great snack or accompaniment to summer salads.
Or you can make them in mini muffin pans and serve them as canapés. What's not to like?
If you love hot, spicy food, add another diced chilli.

MAKES 6–10
PREP 10 MINUTES
COOK 30 MINUTES

Note: If you don't have a 6-hole popover pan just use a standard 12-hole muffin pan in which case the quantities given will make approximately 9–10 popovers.

125g (4oz/1¼ cups) plain (all-purpose) flour
½ tsp salt
3 large free-range eggs
240ml (8fl oz/1 cup) milk
5 tbsp melted butter
25g (1oz/¼ cup) grated Cheddar cheese
1 jalapeño pepper, deseeded and diced
2 tbsp finely chopped parsley

Preheat the oven to 220°C (200°C fan)/425°F/gas 7.

Make the batter: sift the flour into a bowl and stir in the salt. Beat together the eggs, milk and 2 tablespoons of the melted butter with a balloon whisk or hand-held electric whisk. Gradually add the liquid mixture to the flour, beating all the time, until you have a smooth batter without any lumps. Stir in the cheese, jalapeño and parsley.

Put a little melted butter in each cup of a 6-cup straight-sided popover pan or a 12-cup muffin pan. Place in the hot oven for 5 minutes, or until the butter starts to sizzle.

Quickly pour the batter into the cups (about halfway up) and bake for 15 minutes. Reduce the heat to 180°C (160°C fan)/350°F/gas 4 and bake for a further 15 minutes, or until the popovers are crisp, puffed up and golden brown. Do not open the oven door while the popovers are cooking or they may collapse.

Remove the popovers from the pan and, to enjoy them at their best, eat them piping hot.

VARIATIONS
- You can use any chillies, e.g. bird's eye, habanero or Scotch bonnet.
- Use grated Gruyère, Monterey Jack or any hard cheese.
- Substitute chives for parsley.
- Add some finely chopped spring onions (scallions).

SWEET TREATS AND DESSERTS

BANOFFEE TOAD IN THE HOLE

//

It's easy to transform a basic Yorkshire batter into a sexy dessert. Just add bananas and chocolate and serve with caramel sauce or dulce de leche.

SERVES 4
PREP 15 MINUTES
STAND 15–30 MINUTES
COOK 25–30 MINUTES

30g (1oz/2 tbsp) unsalted butter
1 tbsp vegetable oil
2 large bananas, peeled and
    halved lengthways
150g (5oz) milk chocolate,
    broken into chunks
icing (confectioner's) sugar,
    for dusting
caramel sauce, for drizzling
pouring cream or custard,
    to serve

BATTER
175g (6oz/1¾ cups) plain
    (all-purpose) flour
¼ tsp salt
50g (2oz/¼ cup) soft brown sugar
4 large free-range eggs, beaten
420ml (14fl oz/1¾ cups) milk
1 tsp vanilla extract

Preheat the oven to 200°C (180°C fan)/400°F/gas 6.

Make the batter: sift the flour and salt into a bowl. Stir in the sugar and make a well in the centre. Add the eggs with a little of the milk. Beat together and then gradually beat in the rest of the milk and the vanilla extract until you have a smooth batter without any lumps. Transfer to a jug and set aside to stand for 15–30 minutes.

Put the butter and oil in a large roasting pan or ovenproof dish (about 30 x 25cm (12 x 10 inches) and place on a high shelf in the hot oven for about 5–10 minutes, or until the fat is sizzling and smoking.

Quickly place the bananas, cut-side up, in the pan and pour in the batter. Sprinkle with the chocolate and bake in the oven for 25–30 minutes, or until well-risen, crisp and golden brown. Do not open the oven door while the pudding is cooking or it may collapse.

Remove from the oven and dust with icing sugar. Cut into 4 pieces and serve immediately, drizzled with caramel sauce, with cream or custard.

VARIATIONS
· Use 4 whole small bananas instead of 2 halved large ones if preferred.
· Drizzle the pudding with dulce de leche.

HEDGEROW YORKSHIRES

//

This is the perfect hot dessert for cooler autumnal (fall) days, when apples are in season and the hedgerows are laden with the new crop of blackberries. You can cook the apples and make the batter in advance, if wished.

SERVES 6
PREP 15 MINUTES
COOK 25–30 MINUTES

25g (1oz/2 tbsp) unsalted butter
4 dessert apples, peeled, cored
    and cubed
2–3 tbsp caster (superfine) sugar
100g (4oz/1 cup) blackberries
12 tsp vegetable oil
icing (confectioner's) sugar,
    for dusting
cream, crème fraîche or ice
    cream, to serve

BATTER
175g (6oz/1¾ cups) plain
    (all-purpose) flour
¼ tsp salt
50g (2oz/¼ cup) caster
    (superfine) sugar
3 large free-range eggs, beaten
200ml (7 fl oz/scant 1 cup) milk

Preheat the oven to 220°C (200°C fan)/425°F/gas 7.

Make the batter: sift the flour and salt into a bowl and stir in the sugar. Whisk in the beaten eggs and a little of the milk. Gradually whisk in the remaining milk until you have a smooth batter without any lumps. Pour into a jug and set aside.

Melt the butter in a saucepan set over a medium heat. Add the apples and cook, stirring occasionally, for 5 minutes, or until just tender and golden. Stir the sugar into the apples and then add to the batter with the blackberries.

Put a teaspoon of oil in each cup of a 12-hole muffin pan and place in the preheated oven for 5–10 minutes until the oil is sizzling and starting to smoke.

Quickly ladle the batter into the pan, distributing the fruit evenly among the cups. Cook in the oven for 20–25 minutes, or until well-risen, puffy and golden brown. Do not open the oven door while the puddings are cooking or they may collapse.

Serve, dusted with icing sugar, with some cream, crème fraîche or ice cream.

VARIATIONS
· Use blueberries or raspberries instead of blackberries.
· If you don't have any apples, use chunky apple sauce instead.

APPLE CRUMBLE YORKSHIRE PUDDING

//

Who would have thought that you could transform a humble Yorkshire into a delicious apple crumble with a crunchy topping? And it's so easy.

SERVES 4
PREP 15 MINUTES
COOK 20–25 MINUTES

Note: You will need a non-stick deep 4-cup 23cm (9 inch) square Yorkshire pudding pan.

4 tsp vegetable oil
25g (1oz/2 tbsp) unsalted butter
4 dessert apples, peeled, cored and cubed
2–3 tbsp caster (superfine) sugar
a good pinch of ground cinnamon
50g (2oz/½ cup) granola
4 tbsp toasted almonds
cream, crème fraîche or ice cream, to serve

BATTER
125g (4½oz/1¼ cups) plain (all-purpose) flour
¼ tsp salt
1 tbsp caster (superfine) sugar
3 large free-range eggs, beaten
240ml (8fl oz/1 cup) milk

Preheat the oven to 220°C (200°C fan)/425°F/gas 7.

Make the batter: sift the flour and salt into a bowl and stir in the sugar. Beat in the eggs and a little milk. Gradually whisk in the remaining milk until you have a smooth batter without any lumps. Transfer to a jug.

Put 1 teaspoon vegetable oil in each of the 4 cups in the Yorkshire pudding pan and place in the preheated oven for 5–10 minutes, until the oil is smoking and sizzling hot.

Quickly pour the batter into the cups and place in the oven immediately. Bake for 20–25 minutes, or until well-risen and golden brown. Do not open the oven door while the pudding is cooking or it may collapse.

Meanwhile, melt the butter in a saucepan set over a low to medium heat. Add the apples and cook, stirring occasionally, for 10 minutes, or until they are tender and golden. Stir in the sugar (to taste) and cinnamon.

Fill the Yorkshires with the buttery apples and sprinkle with the granola and toasted almonds. Serve immediately with cream, crème fraîche or ice cream.

VARIATIONS
- Flavour the apples with lemon zest and juice instead of cinnamon.
- Instead of granola, top the filled Yorkshires with some crumble topping mix and pop back in the oven for about 10–15 minutes until cooked and browned.

YORKSHIRE PUDDING PROFITEROLES

//

It's amazing that you can turn individual Yorkshires into delicious profiteroles. We have used a 12-hole muffin pan, but you could use a 24-hole mini muffin pan and make bite-sized Yorkshires.

SERVES 6
PREP 15 MINUTES
STAND 15–30 MINUTES
COOK 20–25 MINUTES

12 tsp vegetable oil
100g (4oz) dark chocolate
   (70% cocoa solids), broken
   into squares
30g (1oz/2 tbsp) butter
2 tbsp golden (corn) syrup
300ml (½ pint/1¼ cups) double
   (heavy) cream
2 tbsp icing (confectioner's) sugar
½ tsp vanilla extract

BATTER
225g (8oz/2¼ cups) plain
   (all-purpose) flour
¼ tsp salt
1 tbsp caster (superfine) sugar
4 large free-range eggs, beaten
300ml (½ pint/1¼ cups) milk

Preheat the oven to 220°C (200°C fan)/425°F/gas 7.

Make the batter: sift the flour and salt into a bowl. Stir in the sugar and make a well in the centre. Add the eggs with a little of the milk. Beat together and then gradually beat in the rest of the milk until you have a smooth batter without any lumps. Transfer to a jug and leave to stand for 15–30 minutes.

Put 1 teaspoon oil in each cup in a 12-hole muffin pan and place on a high shelf in the hot oven for 5–10 minutes, or until the oil is sizzling and smoking.

Quickly pour the batter into the cups and bake in the hot oven for 20–25 minutes, or until well-risen, crisp and golden brown. Do not open the oven door while the puddings are cooking or they may collapse. Leave the Yorkshires to cool for 5 minutes.

Meanwhile, put the chocolate, butter and syrup in a heatproof bowl suspended over a pan of gently simmering water. Heat, stirring occasionally, until the chocolate and butter melt. Add 2 tablespoons of the cream and stir until smooth. Remove from the heat.

Whip the remaining cream with the icing sugar and vanilla extract until it stands in stiff peaks.

Put 2 Yorkshires on each serving plate and fill each one with whipped cream. Drizzle with the chocolate sauce and serve immediately while they are still warm.

VARIATIONS
• Drizzle the Yorkshires with melted chocolate, caramel sauce or dulce de leche.
• Add some vanilla to the Yorkshire batter.

YORKSHIRE PUDDING CUSTARD TARTS

//

Instead of using pastry tart cases, why not use crisp and golden Yorkshires as a delicious alternative? They are so easy to make and everyone will love them.

SERVES 4
PREP 20 MINUTES
COOK 25–35 MINUTES

Note: You will need a non-stick deep 4-cup 23cm (9 inch) square Yorkshire pudding pan.

4 tsp vegetable oil
2 tbsp custard powder
4 tbsp caster (superfine) sugar
480ml (16fl oz/2 cups) milk
icing (confectioner's) sugar,
    for dusting
ground nutmeg, for dusting
100g (4oz/1 cup) fresh
    raspberries, blackberries
    or blueberries

BATTER
125g (4½oz/1¼ cups) plain
    (all-purpose) flour
¼ tsp salt
1 tbsp caster (superfine) sugar
3 large free-range eggs, beaten
240ml (8fl oz/1 cup) milk

Preheat the oven to 220°C (200°C fan)/425°F/gas 7.

Make the batter: sift the flour and salt into a bowl and stir in the sugar. Beat in the eggs and a little milk. Gradually whisk in the remaining milk until you have a smooth batter without any lumps. Transfer to a jug.

Put 1 teaspoon vegetable oil in each of the 4 cups in the Yorkshire pudding pan and place in the preheated oven for 5–10 minutes, until the oil is smoking and sizzling hot.

Quickly pour the batter into the cups and place in the oven immediately. Bake for 20–25 minutes, or until well-risen and golden brown. Do not open the oven door while the puddings are cooking or they may collapse.

Meanwhile, make the custard (unless you are using ready-made custard – see below). Put the custard powder and 2 tablespoons of the sugar in a bowl and add enough milk (2–3 tablespoons) to mix to a smooth paste. Heat the remaining milk in a pan over a high heat until it is really hot and just starting to boil. Remove from the heat immediately and stir into the custard powder mixture until smooth. Return to the pan and stir continuously over a medium to high heat until the custard starts to boil and thickens.

Pour the custard into the baked Yorkshires and sprinkle the remaining sugar over the top. Dust with nutmeg and bake in the oven for 5–10 minutes, until starting to brown on top.

Dust with icing sugar and serve immediately with fresh berries and any leftover pouring custard.

Tip: Instead of making the custard, use ready-made (available in the chilled cabinets in supermarkets). Just heat through and pour into the Yorkshires before baking.

MARS BAR YORKSHIRES

//

This dessert is a real treat – golden Yorkshires oozing with hot chocolate
and caramel Mars Bars. They are irresistible.

SERVES 6
PREP 10 MINUTES
STAND 15–30 MINUTES
COOK 20–25 MINUTES

12 tsp vegetable oil
2 x 50g (2oz) Mars Bars, sliced
icing (confectioner's) sugar, for
    dusting
caramel sauce and pouring
    cream, to serve

BATTER
175g (6oz/1¾ cups) plain
    (all-purpose) flour
¼ tsp salt
1 tbsp soft brown sugar
3 large free-range eggs, beaten
200ml (7fl oz/scant 1 cup) milk
1 tsp vanilla extract

Preheat the oven to 220°C (200°C fan)/425°F/gas 7.

Make the batter: sift the flour and salt into a bowl. Stir in the
sugar and make a well in the centre. Add the eggs with a little
of the milk. Beat together and then gradually beat in the rest of
the milk and the vanilla extract until you have a smooth batter
without any lumps. Transfer to a jug and set aside to stand for
15–30 minutes.

Put 1 teaspoon oil in each cup in a 12-hole muffin pan and place
on a high shelf in the hot oven for 5–10 minutes, or until the oil
is sizzling and smoking.

Quickly pour the batter into the cups and add some chopped
Mars Bar to each one. Bake in the hot oven for 20–25 minutes,
or until well-risen, crisp and golden brown. Do not open the oven
door while the puddings are cooking or they may collapse.

Remove from the oven and dust with icing sugar. Serve
immediately, drizzled with caramel sauce, with some cream.

VARIATIONS
- Serve with chocolate sauce or custard.
- Serve hot with vanilla ice cream and seasonal berries.
- Try making these puddings with your favourite
  chocolate bars.

DUTCH BABY CHERRY YORKSHIRES

//

This billowing soft pancake made with a Yorkshire-style batter is an all-American favourite.
The juicy cherries nestling inside make it extra sweet and irresistible.

SERVES 4
PREP 15 MINUTES
COOK 20–30 MINUTES

4 tbsp butter
400g (14oz/1¾ cups) cherries,
   stoned (pitted)
2 tbsp Demerara (raw) sugar
toasted flaked almonds,
   for sprinkling
icing (confectioner's) sugar,
   for dusting
cream or vanilla ice cream,
   to serve

BATTER
75g (3oz/¾ cup) plain
   (all purpose) flour
¼ tsp salt
1 tsp ground cinnamon
3 large free-range eggs
200ml (7fl oz/scant 1 cup) milk
1 tsp vanilla extract
2 tbsp melted butter

Preheat the oven to 220°C (200°C fan)/425°F/gas 7.

Put the butter, the cherries and sugar in a 25cm (10 inch) ovenproof heavy cast-iron frying pan (skillet). Place in the oven for 6–8 minutes, or until the cherries have softened and the butter is really hot. Stir to dissolve the sugar.

Meanwhile, use a hand-held electric whisk or a food mixer to make the batter: beat the flour, salt, cinnamon, eggs, milk, vanilla extract and melted butter until you have a smooth batter without any lumps. Transfer to a jug.

Quickly pour the batter over the cherries in the hot pan and return to the oven. Bake for 15–20 minutes, or until well-risen, puffy and golden brown. Do not open the oven door while the pudding is cooking or it may collapse.

Sprinkle with toasted flaked almonds and dust with icing sugar. Serve immediately, cut into slices, with cream or ice cream.

Tip: If you prefer, you can cook the cherries with the butter and sugar on the hob instead of placing the pan in the oven.

VARIATIONS
- Add 1 tablespoon amaretto, kirsch or brandy to the cherries, sugar and butter.
- Drizzle the pancake with maple syrup or honey.
- Use soft brown sugar instead of Demerara.

PEACHES AND CREAM YORKSHIRE PUDDING

//

This Yorkshire dessert is our take on the classic American 'Dutch baby', which is a sort of pancake cooked in the oven and served with fruit and cream. If you don't have an ovenproof frying pan, use a roasting pan.

SERVES 4
PREP 15 MINUTES
COOK 10 MINUTES

4 tbsp butter
2 ripe peaches, stoned (pitted)
    and thinly sliced
2 tbsp Demerara (raw) sugar
icing (confectioner's) sugar,
    for dusting
whipped cream, to serve

BATTER

75g (3oz/¾ cup) plain
    (all purpose) flour
¼ tsp salt
1 tsp ground cinnamon
3 large free-range eggs
200ml (7fl oz/scant 1 cup) milk
1 tsp vanilla extract
2 tbsp melted butter

CINNAMON SUGAR

2 tbsp Demerara (raw) sugar
1 tsp ground cinnamon

Preheat the oven to 220°C (200°C fan)/425°F/gas 7.

Put the butter, peaches and sugar in a 25cm (10 inch) ovenproof heavy cast-iron frying pan (skillet). Place in the oven for about 6–8 minutes, or until the peaches are softened and the butter has browned. Stir to dissolve the sugar.

Meanwhile, use a hand-held electric whisk or a food mixer to make the batter: beat the flour, salt, cinnamon, eggs, milk, vanilla extract and melted butter until you have a smooth batter without any lumps. Transfer to a jug.

Quickly pour the batter into the hot pan and return to the oven. Bake for 20 minutes, or until well-risen, puffy and golden brown. Do not open the oven door while the pudding is cooking or it may collapse.

Stir the sugar and cinnamon together and sprinkle over the Yorkshire. Dust with icing sugar and serve immediately, cut into slices, with whipped cream.

VARIATIONS
· Use pears or apples instead of peaches.
· Drizzle with maple syrup.

CINNAMON CHURRO POPOVERS

///

These easy-to-make popovers are coated with cinnamon-flavoured sugar. If you don't want to whisk them by hand, just blitz everything for the batter in a blender until smooth. If you don't have a popover pan just use a standard muffin pan, in which case the quantities given will make 10–12 popovers.

MAKES 6–12
PREP 15 MINUTES
COOK 30 MINUTES

BATTER

125g (4½oz/1¼ cups) plain
   (all-purpose) flour
½ tsp baking powder
1 tsp caster (superfine) sugar
½ tsp salt
3 large free-range eggs
240ml (8fl oz/1 cup) milk
2 tbsp melted butter, plus extra
   for brushing

CINNAMON SUGAR COATING

125g (4½oz/generous ½ cup)
   caster (superfine) sugar
1 tsp ground cinnamon
4 tbsp melted unsalted butter

Preheat the oven to 220°C (200°C fan)/425°F/gas 7.

Make the batter: sift the flour and baking powder into a bowl and stir in the sugar and salt. Beat together the eggs, milk and melted butter with a balloon whisk or hand-held electric whisk. Gradually add the liquid mixture to the flour, stirring all the time, until you have a smooth batter without any lumps. Transfer to a jug.

Place a 6-cup straight-sided popover pan or a 12-cup muffin pan in the hot oven for 5 minutes. Remove and brush each cup with the hot melted butter.

Quickly pour the batter into the cups and bake in the oven for 15 minutes. Reduce the heat to 180°C (160°C fan)/350°F/gas 4 and bake for a further 15 minutes, or until well-risen, crisp and golden brown. Do not open the oven door while the popovers are cooking or they may collapse. Leave in the pan for 5 minutes, then remove the popovers and place on a wire rack until they are just cool enough to handle but still warm.

Mix the sugar and cinnamon together on a plate. Brush the warm popovers with melted butter and roll them in the cinnamon sugar. Eat immediately while they are still at their best.

VARIATIONS
· If you don't like cinnamon, just roll the popovers in sugar.
· Dip the popovers in chocolate sauce or dulce de leche.

BANANA AND NUTELLA YORKSHIRE WRAPS

//

You will need an ovenproof frying pan (skillet) to make these delicious wraps – don't use one with a wooden handle.

SERVES 4
PREP 15 MINUTES
STAND 15 MINUTES
COOK 40 MINUTES

4 tsp vegetable oil
45g (1½oz/3 tbsp) unsalted
  butter
2 tsp clear honey
2 bananas, peeled and halved
  lengthways
4 tbsp Nutella or chocolate
  spread (at room temperature)
4 tsp chopped almonds or
  walnuts
whipped cream or ice cream,
  to serve

BATTER

125g (4½oz/1¼ cups) plain
  (all-purpose) flour
¼ tsp salt
3 large free-range eggs, beaten
300ml (½ pint/1¼ cups) milk

Preheat the oven to 220°C (200°C fan)/425°F/gas 7.

Make the batter: sift the flour and salt into a bowl. Beat in the eggs and a little milk. Gradually whisk in the remaining milk until you have a smooth batter. Transfer to a jug and stand for 15 minutes.

Heat a 20cm (8 inch) ovenproof frying pan (skillet) near the top of the oven until it's really hot. Remove and place on top of the hob over a high heat. Add 1 teaspoon oil and as soon as it starts to sizzle and smoke, quickly pour in one-quarter of the batter. Tilt the pan to swirl it around and cover the base evenly.

Return the pan to the oven and cook for 5 minutes. Remove and carefully turn the Yorkshire wrap over. Pop back into the oven for another 5 minutes, or until puffy, set and golden brown. Slide out of the pan and place on a plate. Cover with foil and set aside to soften while you cook the other 3 wraps in the same way.

Meanwhile, heat the butter and honey in a frying pan (skillet) set over a medium heat and cook the bananas for 3–4 minutes each side until golden brown and softened.

Spread the Nutella or chocolate spread over the cooked Yorkshire pancakes and place a banana slice on top of each one. Sprinkle with nuts and add some whipped cream or ice cream. Fold over or roll up and serve immediately.

VARIATIONS
· Instead of Nutella or chocolate spread, sprinkle with
  grated or chopped chocolate.
· Serve drizzled with honey, maple syrup or chocolate sauce.
· Use chopped pistachios or flaked almonds.
· Dust the wraps with icing (confectioner's) sugar.

SCANDINAVIAN PANCAKE WITH RED BERRY COMPÔTE

This delicious pancake is a Yorkshire hybrid, slightly flatter than the traditional pudding but made in the same way. If fresh berries are not in season, you can use frozen ones instead.

SERVES 4
PREP 10 MINUTES
STAND 15 MINUTES
COOK 25 MINUTES

25g (1oz/2 tbsp) butter
400g (14oz/4 cups) mixed
    red berries, e.g. redcurrants,
    raspberries or quartered small
    strawberries
50g (2oz/¼ cup) caster
    (superfine) sugar
icing (confectioner's sugar),
    for dusting
soured cream, to serve

BATTER
125g (4½oz/1¼ cups) plain
    (all-purpose) flour
1 tsp baking powder
¼ tsp salt
2 tbsp caster (superfine) sugar
3 large free-range eggs, beaten
300ml (½ pint/1¼ cups) milk

Preheat the oven to 220°C (200°C fan)/425°F/gas 7.

Make the batter: sift the flour, baking powder and salt into a bowl and stir in the sugar. Whisk in the beaten eggs and a little of the milk. Gradually whisk in the remaining milk until you have a smooth batter without any lumps. Pour into a jug and set aside for about 15 minutes.

Put the butter in a large roasting pan or ovenproof baking dish and place in the oven for 5 minutes until the butter melts and the pan is really hot.

Quickly pour the batter into the hot pan and bake in the oven for 25 minutes, or until well-risen and golden brown. Do not open the oven door while the pudding is cooking or it may collapse.

Meanwhile, make the compôte: put the berries and caster sugar in a saucepan with 2 tablespoons water. Bring to the boil, stirring all the time until the sugar dissolves, then reduce the heat to low and simmer gently for 5 minutes. Pour into a serving bowl and set aside.

Dust the Yorkshire pancake with icing sugar and cut into 4 slabs. Serve immediately with the red berry compôte and soured cream.

VARIATIONS
· Add a few drops of vanilla extract to the batter.
· Serve with crème fraîche or whipped cream.
· Flavour the compôte with a vanilla pod.

SICILIAN RICOTTA POPOVERS

//

These buttery popovers are allowed to cool a little and then are filled with a fabulous sweet ricotta mixture, which is usually used for stuffing cannoli.

MAKES 6–10
PREP 15 MINUTES
COOK 30–35 MINUTES

Note: If you don't have a 6-hole popover pan just use a standard 12-hole muffin pan in which case the quantities given will make approximately 9–10 popovers.

BATTER
125g (4½oz/1¼ cups) plain (all-purpose) flour
1 tsp caster (superfine) sugar
½ tsp salt
3 large free-range eggs
240ml (8fl oz/1 cup) milk
2 tbsp melted butter, plus extra for brushing

RICOTTA FILLING
150g (5oz/scant ¾ cup) ricotta
50g (2oz/¼ cup) mascarpone
1 tbsp icing (confectioner's) sugar
2 tbsp diced candied peel
2 tbsp dark chocolate chips
icing (confectioner's) sugar, for dusting (optional)

Preheat the oven to 220°C (200°C fan)/425°F/gas 7.

Make the batter: sift the flour into a bowl and stir in the sugar and salt. Beat together the eggs, milk and melted butter with a balloon whisk or hand-held electric whisk. Gradually add the liquid mixture to the flour, stirring all the time, until you have a smooth batter without any lumps. Transfer to a jug.

Place a 6-cup straight-sided popover pan or a 12-cup muffin pan in the hot oven for 5 minutes. Remove and brush each cup with the hot melted butter.

Quickly pour the batter into the cups and bake in the middle of the oven for 15 minutes. Reduce the heat to 180°C (160°C fan)/350°F/gas 4 and bake for a further 15 minutes, or until well-risen, crisp and golden brown. Do not open the oven door while the popovers are cooking or they may collapse. Leave in the pan for 5 minutes, then remove the popovers and place on a wire rack until they are just cool enough to handle but still warm.

While the popovers are cooking, make the ricotta filling: place the ricotta and mascarpone in a bowl and beat until well combined. Stir in the icing sugar, candied peel and chocolate chips.

Fill the popovers with the ricotta filling and serve, dusted with icing sugar, with any leftover ricotta on the side.

VARIATIONS
· Drizzle the filled popovers with chocolate sauce.
· Add some chopped pistachios to the filling.

NUTELLA YORKSHIRE POPOVERS

///

If you like chocolate, you'll love these popovers. They are so easy to make in a blender or
food mixer but don't worry if you don't have one – just tip everything into a bowl
and use a hand-held electric whisk.

MAKES 6–10
PREP 15 MINUTES
COOK 30 MINUTES

Note: If you don't have a 6-hole
popover pan just use a standard
12-hole muffin pan in which case
the quantities given will make
approximately 9–10 popovers.

BATTER
125g (4½oz/1¼ cups) plain
    (all-purpose) flour
1 tbsp cocoa powder
1 tbsp caster (superfine) sugar
½ tsp salt
3 large free-range eggs
240ml (8fl oz/1 cup) milk
3 tbsp Nutella
1 tsp vanilla extract
2 tbsp melted unsalted butter,
    plus extra for brushing

TO SERVE
icing (confectioner's) sugar,
    for dusting
whipped cream or ice cream,
    to serve

Preheat the oven to 220°C (200°C fan)/425°F/gas 7.

Use a food mixer, food processor or blender to make the batter:
sift the flour and cocoa into the bowl and add the sugar, salt,
eggs, milk, Nutella, vanilla extract and melted butter. Blitz or
beat until you have a smooth batter without any lumps. Transfer
to a jug and set aside.

Place a 6-cup straight-sided popover pan or a 12-cup muffin
pan in the hot oven for 5 minutes. Remove and brush each cup
with hot melted butter.

Quickly pour the batter into the cups and bake in the middle
of the oven for 15 minutes. Reduce the heat to 180°C (160°C
fan)/350°F/gas 4 and bake for a further 15 minutes, or until
well-risen, crisp and brown. Do not open the oven door while the
popovers cooking or they may collapse.

Serve the popovers, lightly dusted with icing sugar, immediately
with some whipped cream or ice cream.

VARIATIONS
· Dust the popovers with cocoa powder.
· Serve with chilled Greek yoghurt and raspberries.

MEXICAN CHOCOLATE POPOVERS

Eat these gently spiced chocolate popovers at teatime or serve for dessert with fruit and cream. If you have a very sweet tooth you may wish to add more sugar. If you don't have a popover pan, use a standard muffin pan in which case the quantities given will make 9–10 popovers.

MAKES 6–12
PREP 10 MINUTES
COOK 30 MINUTES

125g (4½oz/1¼ cups) plain (all-purpose) flour
25g (1oz/¼ cup) cocoa powder
1 tsp ground cinnamon
a pinch of chilli powder
½ tsp salt
2 tbsp caster (superfine) sugar
3 large free-range eggs
240ml (8fl oz/1 cup) milk
2 tbsp melted unsalted butter, plus extra for brushing
50g (2oz/¼ cup) chocolate chips

Preheat the oven to 220°C (200°C fan)/425°F/gas 7.

Make the batter: sift the flour and cocoa into a bowl and stir in the cinnamon, chilli powder, salt and sugar. Beat together the eggs, milk and melted butter with a balloon whisk or hand-held electric whisk. Gradually add the liquid mixture to the flour, beating all the time, until you have a smooth batter without any lumps. Stir in the chocolate chips and transfer to a jug.

Place a 6-cup straight-sided popover pan or a 12-cup muffin pan in the hot oven for 5 minutes. Remove and brush each cup with the hot melted butter.

Quickly pour the batter into the cups and bake in the middle of the oven for 15 minutes. Reduce the heat to 180°C (160°C fan)/350°F/gas 4 and bake for a further 15 minutes, or until well-risen, crisp and puffy. Do not open the oven door while the popovers are cooking or they may collapse.

Remove the popovers from the pan and serve immediately.

VARIATIONS
· Serve with cream, crème fraîche or vanilla ice cream.
· Dust with cocoa or icing (confectioner's) sugar.
· Serve with fresh fruit and Greek yoghurt.

INDEX